God's BIG Story

God's BIG Story

Reading | Level 2

By R.A. Sheats

Illustrations by Zakir Hussain

Generations

PASSING ON THE FAITH

ISBN: 978-1-954745-01-8

Cover Design: Justin Turley
Cover Illustration: Matthew Sample II
Interior Layout Design: Sarah Lee Bryant

Published by:
Generations
19039 Plaza Drive Ste 210
Parker, Colorado 80134
www.generations.org

For more information on this and
other titles from Generations,
visit www.generations.org or call 888-389-9080.

CONTENTS

TO THE PARENT
AND TEACHER

Welcome to *God's Big Story*! It is our joy to partner with you in the glorious task of introducing young minds to the eternal truths contained in the Word of our gracious and loving God.

This coursework is intended to serve as an aid to parents who are looking for a Christian Family Discipleship approach to the education of their children. Christian education is always parent integrated, Bible integrated, and life integrated. This is the clear philosophy of education visible in Deuteronomy 6:6-9, Ephesians 6:4, and the book of Proverbs. *God's Big Story* seeks to follow this biblical mandate by introducing children to Scripture and to the faith and life lessons to be gleaned from it. This curriculum focuses on nurturing children in the faith, in Christ, and in Christian character. Every chapter of this reading course will familiarize students with a new historical passage from Scripture and will teach the child how to learn from and apply the truths contained in each biblical account.

Best Book Approach

Nowadays it's fashionable to introduce "great books" to our children in their Christian *paideia* or educational training. We, however, recommend the best Book—the Bible. If our children want to learn to read and think, the first and core content of their study must be the Bible. These are God's stories, and our children should know all the stories of Scripture by the time they are reading on a fifth grade level.

Avoiding the piecemeal approach to Bible stories, the authors of this course instead present the whole story, the unity of Scripture, the true message intended by God. It is a redemptive story. While there may be moral lessons to glean here and there, the core message of Scripture is the work of God in redemption. This is the story the Bible presents from cover to cover and is the story that is focused on in this reading course. If our children learn a thousand other stories but miss this one, we have neglected our duty in their education.

The key objectives of this program are:

1. To provide the child with a clear understanding of biblical vocabulary to prepare them to read a substantive English translation of the Bible on their own.
2. To grant the child a familiarity with the full scope of

biblical stories, the historical narrative of God's revelation.

3. To master the entire theme of the Bible, the Christ-focus of Scripture, and the fulfillment of the Old Testament in the New Testament.

4. To believe the Gospel.

5. To worship God, to fear God, and to obey His Word.

Our authors have been careful to present the wide range of Scriptural stories without censorship. However, care has been taken to present stories on a level of understanding appropriate for seven-year-olds.

Scriptural quotations at the end of each chapter are taken from the New King James Version of the Bible. This version has also been used where narratives and conversations in the text include word-for-word Scriptural quotations.

God's Big Story is intended to be used in conjunction with the selection of read-aloud books that form a part of the Generations second grade reading curriculum.

May the Spirit of our God anoint these readings and studies to the spiritual enlightenment, the spiritual life, and the spiritual growth of the students.

Generations Curriculum Team

January 2021

CHAPTER 1

God Creates Everything

When God made the world, He made all things good.

God spoke and **created** all things. He made the light. Then He made the sky and the dry land. He made the grass and the trees and the sun and stars. He made the fish and the birds. Then He made the **animals** that live on the land. He made the lions and zebras and the skunks and mice. He even made the worms and beetles and ants.

God made everything. He saw everything He made, and He said, "It is good."

Then God made man. He formed a man out of the dust of the ground. God breathed into the man and gave him life.

This man was Adam.

Adam saw everything that God had made. He saw the sun and the sky and the grass and the **animals**. God's world was very good.

God saw His world, too. He looked at everything He had made. Then He looked at Adam. Adam was the only man in the world. He was all alone. God said, "It is not good for man to be alone. I will make him a **helper**."

God made Adam fall **asleep**. Then He took a rib out of Adam's side. From this rib God made a woman. Then He gave the woman to Adam.

When Adam saw the woman, he was very happy. God had made the perfect **helper** for Adam. Adam named her Eve.

God made Adam and Eve in His own image. He made them to be with Him and to worship and serve Him. God blessed them and told them, "Have **children** and fill the world I made. Rule over this world. Rule over all the plants and the **animals** and the fish and the birds. I give you every living thing that **moves** on the **earth**."

God saw everything He had made. It was all very good. Now His work of creating was **finished**. Now it was time to rest. On the seventh day, God ended His work and rested. He blessed this day. It is called the Sabbath.

> *Then God blessed them, and God said to them, "Be fruitful and multiply; fill the earth and subdue it; have dominion over the fish of the sea, over the birds of the air, and over every living thing that moves on the earth."*
> *(Genesis 1:28)*

Faith Lessons

God made all things — God made the world and everything in it. This means that all things belong to Him. He owns everything and rules everything. All the world must obey and praise Him. God made us, too. We must obey and praise God, for we belong to Him.

God is a good God — God made the world very good. Everything God makes is good. He is a very good God.

God made a helper for Adam — God saw that Adam was alone. This was not good, so God made Eve. He made man and woman. This is God's good plan. He knows what is good for His world.

God rested on the seventh day — God rested on Day Seven. His world rested on this day, too. This was the Sabbath Day. It was the day God made for us to rest.

Vocabulary

create	asleep	earth
animal	children	finished
helper	move	belong

CHAPTER 2

Sin Brings Death

God gave Adam and Eve an important job to do. He told them, "Have children and rule the world I made." Adam and Eve lived in a garden God had planted for them. They worked in the garden and ruled the plants and animals just like He told them to. This was a **special** job God gave them. They were very happy to do it.

Many trees were in the garden. The trees were tall and green and pretty, and they were full of fruit to eat. God told Adam and Eve they could eat the fruit, but He said, "Don't eat the fruit on the tree in the **middle** of the garden. This tree is not for you. If you eat from it, you will die."

God knew what was good for Adam and Eve, so He gave

them a law to keep them safe. It was a very good law, for all God's laws are very good.

But soon an enemy came creeping and sneaking into the garden. The enemy was **Satan**, and he was very wicked. He didn't want Adam and Eve to obey God, so he came to trick them. He wanted to destroy God's world, so he tried to make Adam and Eve sin and **disobey** God. He wanted Adam and Eve to trust in him, not God.

Satan was tricky. He tried to make Eve think God wasn't good. He told her, "God didn't give you a good law, so you must not obey Him. If you eat the fruit He told you not to, you will not die. You will be just like God!"

Satan lied, but Eve started to think that he was speaking the truth. She looked at the pretty fruit hanging on the tree. Then she said, "It looks very good to eat. Maybe what Satan is saying is true. Maybe God isn't good, and maybe His law isn't a good law." Then she took the fruit and ate it. Adam ate it, too.

When Adam and Eve ate the fruit, they knew Satan had lied to them. Now they knew God's law was good and that they had done a very bad thing. But it was too late. They had disobeyed God, and they had sinned. Now they were very frightened. "We must hide! We must hide from God!" Adam said. He and Eve ran away and hid behind the trees in the garden. They didn't want God to find them.

But God knew where they were. He told Adam, "You didn't obey me. You sinned. Now the work I give you will be hard work. You will have to work hard all your life. Then you will die."

Adam and Eve didn't want to die, but sin brings **death**. This was a very sad day.

But God had mercy on Adam and Eve, too. He said, "You **disobeyed** me and sinned, and you will die. But I will bring a Seed into the world to save you from your sin. He will crush **Satan** and will save you."

Adam and Eve were **frightened**. They were very sad. They hadn't obeyed God. They hadn't obeyed His good law, and now they had sinned. But they trusted God's word. He said He would bring a Seed to save them from sin. One day this Seed would come. One day He would set them free from sin.

> *And I will put enmity*
> *Between you and the woman,*
> *And between your seed and her Seed;*
> *He shall bruise your head,*
> *And you shall bruise His heel.*
> *(Genesis 3:15)*

Faith Lessons

God's Word is good — God gave Adam and Eve a very good law. He knew it was good for them to obey. He gave us the Bible. This is His good law. It teaches us what is good and what is bad. He is a very good God to give us His Word.

Sin brings a curse — The fruit from the tree looked good to Eve, but it was very bad for her. Sin brings a curse with it. We think sin is fun, but it isn't. It will bring a curse. It will always bring very bad things with it.

God will send a Seed — God had mercy on Adam and Eve. He would send a Seed to save them from their sin. This Seed is Jesus Christ. One day He would come to save His people from sin.

Vocabulary

special	disobey	death
middle	knew	
Satan	frightened	

CHAPTER 3

Abel Trusts God

Adam and Eve had a son. They named their son Cain, and they wondered, "Will this be the Seed God promised? Will he save us from our sin?" They didn't know, so they waited and wondered.

Cain had a brother named Abel. Soon the boys grew and became men.

Abel was a good man, but he sinned, too. All people sin. Yet Abel trusted God and asked Him to forgive his sins. Abel wondered, "How can God love us if we sin? How can He be our God if we are wicked people?" Abel knew that God is holy and good and perfect, so He must hate sin. How can we live with God if He hates sin?

Abel said, "I can't stop sinning. I am full of sin. I can't fix my sin, but God can. I must trust God to save me from my sin. I will trust His promises."

All people who sin will die. This is the curse that sin brings on us. But Abel said, "God promised to send a Seed to save me from sin. This Seed will save me from sin's curse."

Abel trusted God to send a Seed. All his life he waited and trusted God.

Abel took care of the animals God made. He had flocks of sheep. One day he took one of his sheep and made an **offering**. He killed the sheep and gave it to God. This was a picture of God's promise. The sheep died, and its blood spilled on the ground. Abel said, "God is **holy** and perfect, and I am sinful. My sin is very black, and God is angry with sin. This sheep will die, and its blood will spill on the ground. Can this sheep's blood clean my sin away? No, it can't. But one day God will make a **sacrifice** that will wash my sins away."

Abel knew the sheep could not wash away his sins. But the sheep was a picture of an **offering** for sin. One day God would make a **sacrifice** to wash sins away. Abel trusted God to do this.

Cain saw what his **brother** Abel did. Cain made an **offering** to God, too. But he didn't trust God, and God was not pleased with his **offering**. This made Cain very angry. He said, "God likes the **offering** that Abel brings, but He is not pleased with my **offering**." What should Cain do? He should be sorry for his sin. He should pray to God and ask Him to save him from sin.

But Cain didn't pray to God. He got very angry. He said, "I will kill my **brother** Abel." Cain went up to Abel and talked to him. Abel didn't know what Cain wanted to do. They walked and talked together, and then Cain killed his **brother**. This was a very wicked thing to do.

After Abel died, God came to Cain. He said, "Where is Abel your **brother**?"

Cain was afraid, so he lied. He said, "I don't know where he is."

But God knew. He saw Cain kill his **brother**. God sees all things and He saw Cain sin, so God cursed Cain.

Now Abel was **dead**, but God would not forget His promise. Abel trusted God, and God would send an **offering** to save Abel from sin.

By faith Abel offered to God a more excellent sacrifice than Cain, through which he obtained witness that he was righteous, God testifying of his gifts; and through it he being dead still speaks.

(Hebrews 11:4)

Faith Lessons

God is holy — Sin is very wicked and brings a curse, so God must punish us for sin. We cannot live with God if we sin. We must die. One day God will judge all the world for sin.

Abel trusted God — Abel was full of sin, but he trusted God. He made an offering for his sin. The sheep's blood could not wash Abel's sins away, but he trusted God to send an offering to save him from sin.

God will make an offering — God promised to send a Seed. This Seed would be a sacrifice for sins. Jesus is this Seed. He would die to be an offering for sin. He would wash away His people's sins.

Vocabulary

wondered	forgive	sacrifice
brother	holy	dead
grew	offering	

CHAPTER 4

Noah Finds Grace

God told Adam and Eve, "Have many children." Adam and Eve obeyed God, and soon the world was full of people. But a big problem filled the world, too. That problem was sin. All of Adam and Eve's children sinned. All of their children's children sinned, too. Everyone on earth sinned.

God saw the people filling the earth. When He made His world it was all very good, but now it was full of sin. Every person on earth was sinning. No one was obeying God. The whole world was full of very wicked people. Men were killing people and doing very wicked things.

Some people tried to follow God and obey Him. But then they looked at the wicked people around them and wanted to be like them, too. Soon all the earth was covered with wicked men and women who hated God.

God looked at the people on the earth. He said, "These people only want to do evil things all the time. I'm sorry that I made them, for they have become very, very wicked. Now I will destroy them all. I will kill everything that I made, both man and animals. I will wipe them all off the face of the earth."

All the earth was filled with sin. It was good for God to destroy all men, for they were all wicked. But God remembered His promise to Adam. He would not destroy all the people. No, He would have mercy on one man. That man was Noah.

God told Noah, "Men and women have become so wicked that I will destroy them all. I will kill them all, and all the animals, too. I'm going to send a flood, and it will kill every living thing on the earth. But I will save you and your family."

God commanded Noah to build an ark for himself and his family. This ark would keep them alive when the flood came. Noah obeyed God and built the ark. Then God sent animals to Noah to put in the ark to protect them from the water.

Then, when the boat was finished, God sent the flood.

Rain came pounding down onto the ground. Waters in the ocean came rushing up to **cover** the **earth**. Soon the **whole** world was **covered** with water. Even the tallest hills and mountains were **covered**.

Water **cover**ed the **earth**, and everything died. God killed the wicked men and women who had filled His **earth** with sin. Only Noah and his family **remained** alive in the ark. God kept them safe in the flood.

After the flood ended, God told Noah and his sons, "Come out of the ark and fill the **earth**. Have many children and rule over the world I made."

Then God sent a rainbow. He told Noah, "This is a **sign** of My **covenant** with you. You are all sinful, but I will have mercy on you. I will never send a flood like this to destroy the world again."

God made a promise to Noah, and He would keep His promise.

> So the Lord said, "I will destroy man whom I have created
> from the face of the earth, both man and beast, creeping
> thing and birds of the air, for I am sorry that I have made
> them." But Noah found grace in the eyes of the Lord.
>
> (Genesis 6:7-8)

Faith Lessons

Sin is very wicked — Sin is a very bad thing. God will punish the world for sin. One day He will judge all people for their sin.

God has mercy — Noah and his sons sinned, but God had mercy on them. He saved them from the flood. He is a very merciful God.

The ark was a picture of Jesus — God sent a flood to destroy the world. No one could live in the flood, but God saved Noah in an ark. This is a picture of Jesus. He came to save His people from sin just like God saved Noah from the flood.

God made a covenant with Noah — God made a promise to Noah. He sent a rainbow as a sign of His promise. Noah trusted that God would keep His promise. God is a true God. He never lies. He will always keep His promises. We can always trust Him.

Vocabulary

earth	protect	sign
whole	cover	covenant
become	remain	merciful

CHAPTER 5

The Lord Confuses Babel

God blessed Noah and his sons and told them to fill the earth. Everything had been destroyed by the flood. Now Noah and his sons had to build new homes and farms. They had many children and began to rebuild on the earth.

But Noah and his sons had a problem. God saved them from the flood, but they were still filled with sin. Their children were filled with sin, too.

Soon the earth was filled with people again. But the people didn't obey God. They kept sinning. They were afraid of God, so they tried to make strong cities to keep them safe. They said, "We don't want to be scattered over all the earth.

Let's make a big city for **ourselves**. We'll make a big tower in the city, too. It will be taller than **anything** on earth."

The people began to build the city and the **huge** tower. They all spoke the same **language**, so they could work together as they built.

God saw what the people were doing, and He was not pleased. He had told the people to fill the earth, but they didn't want to obey Him. They wanted to make their big city and tower and stay there. They didn't think God's commands were good, so they decided to do what they **thought** was **right**.

God knew what was good for His world. He knew it was good for the people to fill the land. He knew it was not good for them to all stay in one place and make a little world of their city. So God said, "I will stop what these wicked people are doing. I will scatter them **across** the whole world. I will confuse their **language**. Then they will not understand each other."

Then God did what He said. He changed the **language** of the people. Soon they were all speaking **different languages**. They didn't know what other people were saying. Everything was confused. Now they couldn't work together on the city or the tower, so they scattered over the whole world just like God said.

> *Therefore its name is called Babel, because there the L*ORD* confused the language of all the earth; and from there the L*ORD* scattered them abroad over the face of all the earth.*
> *(Genesis 11:9)*

Faith Lessons

All people sin — Noah and his sons all sinned. They couldn't stop their sin. Only God has the power to save us from sin.

The people trusted in their city — They didn't trust God. They tried to build a city to keep them safe. But God judged them for their sin. We must not trust in people to keep us safe. We must not trust in strong cities or strong people. We must trust in God.

God judged the people — God will judge wicked men and women. He will judge wicked boys and girls. All people sin, so all people will be judged by God. Only Jesus Christ can save us from our sin.

Vocabulary

ourselves	language	across
anything	thought	different
huge	right	

CHAPTER 6

God Chooses Abram

God scattered the people, and they filled the whole earth. Then one day God chose a man. The man's name was Abram. God told Abram, "Leave your **country** and your home. Come with Me, and I will give you a new land and a new home. I will bless you and make you a big **nation**. I will bless your children, and I will bless all the peoples of the world in you."

Abram **believed** God, so he left his **country** and his home and all his **friends**. Then he took his wife and went to a land far, far away. The land was called **Canaan**. It was filled with wicked people. Abram set up his tent in the land of **Canaan** and lived there.

Then God told Abram, "One day, I will give you this land. I will give you a son, and your children will **possess** this land."

Abram didn't have a son. He didn't have any children. So he said to God, "Lord, how will You give me a son? How will You give me this land? I don't have any children."

God told him, "Come outside." Abram went out of his

tent and looked around. It was night, and darkness covered the land. The only light came from the stars twinkling in the sky above.

Then God said, "Abram, look at the stars. Can you **count** them?"

Abram looked up at the sky. It was filled with stars. There were thousands and thousands of stars! No, he couldn't **count** them. He could never **count** them all!

Then God said, "I will bless you, Abram. I will give you children like the stars. There will be so many children that you will never be able to **count** them all."

Abram looked back up at the stars. Could God do this? Could He make as many children as He had made stars? Abram looked at all the stars twinkling. Then he smiled. Yes, God could do this! He was a strong, **powerful** God. Abram said, "God, I **believe** You. You can do anything. I will trust that You will keep Your promise."

Then God said, "Abram, I will give you a son. He will have sons. Your children and grandchildren will become many people. They will be a **great nation**. When you get old and die, I will take care of your children. Some wicked people will want to hurt them, but I will keep them safe.

Then I will bring them back to this land that I give you. They will live here and will be My people. I will bless people from all **nations** because of My covenant with you." Then God made a covenant with Abram.

God said, "Abram is a man and will sin, but I will have mercy on him. I will keep My covenant with him even when he sins. This is My promise to Abram."

> Then He brought him outside and said, "Look now toward heaven, and count the stars if you are able to number them." And He said to him, "So shall your descendants be." And he believed in the Lord, and He accounted it to him for righteousness.
> (Genesis 15:5-6)

Faith Lessons

God called Abram — All people sin. But God picked Abram. He called him and chose him to be one of His own people. God is merciful. He picks sinful men and women and boys and girls and makes them His people.

God made a covenant — God promised to bless Abram and give him a people and a land. He promised to bless all **nations** in Abram. This is a very good covenant. God even remembered us and our **nation** when He made a covenant with Abram.

Abram believed God — Abram didn't have a son, and he didn't have land. But he **believed** God was true. He trusted that God was **powerful** and good, and he **believed** God would keep His promise. God will always keep His promises. We can trust Him, too.

Vocabulary

country	friend	count
nation	Canaan	powerful
believe	possess	great

CHAPTER 7

Isaac Is Born

Abram and his wife got old. Soon Abram was 99 years old. Then one day God said to him, "Abram, I did not forget My promise. I will still give you a son. I will give you a new name, too. Now your name will be Abraham. You will be a **father** of many nations. I will be your God, and I will be the God of your children, too. This is My covenant that I make with you and with your children after you."

Then God said, "Abraham, you are old, but I will give you a son. He will be born soon."

Abraham's wife Sarah **heard** this. She **laughed** and said, "I'm too old to have a baby!"

But God said, "Why did Sarah **laugh**? Is anything too hard for Me? I will do just what I promised to do. I will keep My word."

Abraham trusted God. Sarah was too old to have a baby, but God kept His promise. He is a powerful God, and He can do anything. Soon Sarah gave birth to a baby boy just like God said she would.

Abraham and Sarah were very happy to have their **little** boy. They named him Isaac. Sarah said, "God has made me **laugh**, and all who hear this will **laugh** with me." She was very glad to be a **mother** to Isaac.

Abraham and Sarah thanked God for their **little** baby. They **watched** as Isaac grew and grew. He **learned** about God and **learned** to obey his **father** and **mother**. Abraham knew this was the son God had promised. God said He would give Abraham a son, and He had kept His promise. Abraham was very glad.

For Sarah conceived and bore Abraham a son in his old age, at the set time of which God had spoken to him. And Abraham called the name of his son who was born to him— whom Sarah bore to him—Isaac.

(Genesis 21:2-3)

Faith Lessons

God kept His promise — Abraham had to wait many years for God to keep His promise. But God didn't forget. He gave him a son just like He said He would.

Abraham and Sarah trusted God — Sarah was too old to have a baby, but she and Abraham trusted God. We can always trust God. His word is true.

Abraham gave glory to God — He trusted God. This gave God glory. When we trust God, we give Him glory, too. He is a great God. We should glorify Him.

Vocabulary

father	little	learn
heard	mother	
laugh	watched	

CHAPTER 8

God Tests Abraham's Faith

One day God tested Abraham. He wanted to show him what **faith** is. **Faith** is trusting in God. It means that we believe His Word. It means we know He will keep His promises.

God said to Abraham, "I want you to make a sacrifice to Me. Take your son, your only son Isaac, whom you love, and go to a mountain I will show you. Then kill Isaac and offer him as a sacrifice to Me."

Abraham obeyed. He called his son Isaac. Then he took some wood and a **knife** and went to the mountain to do what God told him. As he walked to the mountain, he said to **himself**, "God promised to give me a son. He kept His promise and gave me Isaac. I love Isaac very much. But now God is telling me to kill Isaac and give him back to God as an offering. I must obey God. I don't **understand**, but I will obey Him. And I trust that He will keep His promise even if Isaac dies. God is strong. He has great power, and He can bring Isaac back to life and keep His promise."

Abraham trusted God. He knew God could do what He

said He would do.

Soon Abraham and Isaac reached the mountain. Isaac looked at the wood they were carrying. Then he said, "Father, here is the wood, but where is the lamb for the offering?"

Abraham said, "My son, God will provide a lamb."

At the top of the mountain, Abraham made an altar. Then he tied his son Isaac and put him on the altar. Abraham had a sharp knife with him. He took the knife and got ready to kill his son. But then he heard a voice calling him.

God called to him, "Abraham! Do not kill your son! Don't hurt him, for now I know that you fear God. You are willing to obey Me. You are not afraid to trust Me. Don't kill Isaac."

Abraham looked up. Beside the altar was a bush, and in the bush a sheep had gotten stuck. Abraham ran to the sheep and grabbed it. Then he untied his son Isaac and took him off the altar. Then he killed the sheep and offered it on the altar as a sacrifice to God. He praised God and named the top of the mountain. He called it "The Lord Will Provide." God had provided a lamb!

*By faith Abraham, when he was tested, offered up Isaac,
and he who had received the promises offered up his only
begotten son, of whom it was said, "In Isaac your seed shall
be called," concluding that God was able to raise him up,
even from the dead.
(Hebrews 11:17-19)*

Faith Lessons

God showed Abraham what faith was — Abraham trusted God. But he learned to trust God even more when God told him to do a very hard thing. God was pleased with Abraham. He was a man of faith, and he was a man who feared God.

Abraham believed God — He knew that God would keep His promise. He trusted that God had the power to bring Isaac back to life if he died.

God teaches us in history — Abraham learned how to trust God. God teaches us to trust Him in this history, too. We learn from this that God is strong and that He keeps His promises. We must trust Him. We must have faith like Abraham did.

God provided a lamb — God made a sheep get stuck in the bush so Abraham could sacrifice it. Later on, God would send a perfect Lamb. This Lamb would die as an offering for sin. This Lamb was Jesus Christ.

Vocabulary

faith	understand	altar
knife	carrying	ready
himself	lamb	

CHAPTER 9

Finding a Godly Wife for Isaac

After Isaac became a man, Abraham said, "God promised to bless my son and his children. I must find a godly wife for Isaac. He needs a wife who fears God. She will help him **raise** a godly family who will fear and obey God."

Abraham was a very rich man. God had blessed him with flocks and herds. He had given him much silver and gold. Now Abraham called one of his **servants**. He trusted this man and he told him, "Isaac needs a wife. Go back to where my family lives. It is far, far away. Find a girl there who fears God and who will come be a wife for Isaac."

The **servant** obeyed Abraham. He gathered many camels

and some men. Then he started on the long journey. He traveled many days before he reached a town where Abraham's family lived.

When they got to the town, the servant stopped at the well. He was thirsty and his camels were thirsty, but he didn't take water from the well. He waited and prayed, "God, please send a woman to be a wife for Isaac. Let her come and draw water from the well. Let her offer to get water for me and my men and camels. Then I will know that You have sent her."

While he prayed, a woman came to the well. She carried a pitcher on her shoulder. She went to the well and filled it with water. Then she turned to go home. But the servant ran up to her and said, "Please let me have a drink."

The woman's name was Rebekah. She gave the man a drink and said, "Drink, sir. Then I will draw water for all your camels, too." She ran back to the well and drew more water. She kept bringing water until all the camels had finished drinking. As she worked, the man waited and wondered, "Is this the wife for Isaac?"

When Rebekah was finished, the man asked, "Who are you?"

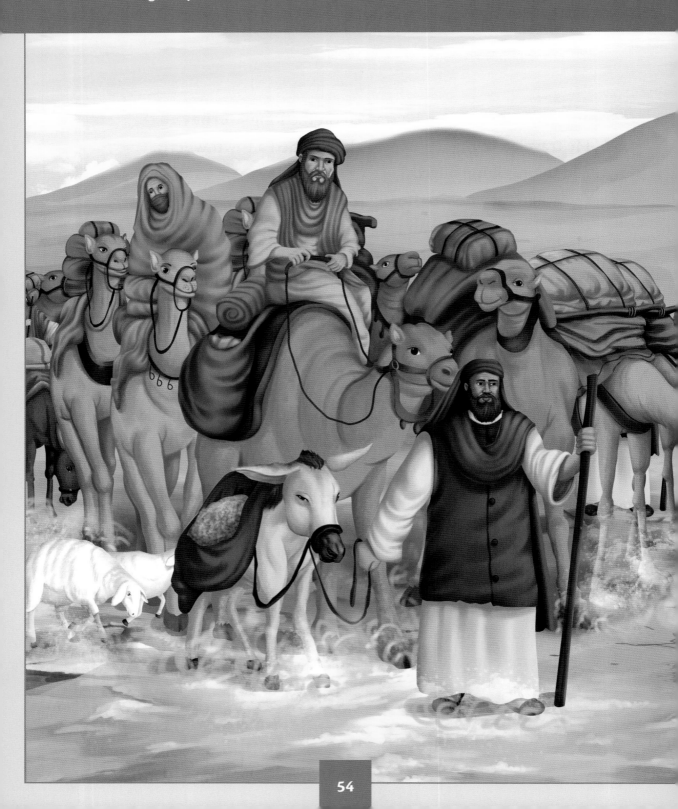

Rebekah said, "I am the daughter of Bethuel." Then the servant knew that she was part of Abraham's family. He was filled with joy and worshiped God.

He said, "God is very good! He shows mercy to my master Abraham! He has sent a woman from Abraham's family to be a wife for Isaac!"

> *Then the man bowed down his head and worshiped the Lord. And he said, "Blessed be the Lord God of my master Abraham, who has not forsaken His mercy and His truth toward my master."*
> *(Genesis 24:26-27)*

Faith Lessons

Isaac needed a godly wife — Abraham loved God. He knew his son needed a godly wife. She had to be a woman who feared God. This was what God commanded.

The servant trusted God — The servant knew God could find a godly wife. He prayed that God would send the right girl. God did. He sent a good wife for Isaac. God is full of mercy for those who trust Him.

God takes care of little things — The world was filled with many, many people. Isaac was only one little person. But God didn't forget him. He took care of him and sent him a good wife. God made all the world and everything in it. He takes care of it all, even the small things.

Vocabulary

raise	thirsty	worship
servant	pitcher	
journey	daughter	

CHAPTER 10

Esau Gives His Birthright to Jacob

God blessed Isaac and Rebekah. Isaac prayed for children, and God heard his prayer. Soon Rebekah became **pregnant**. But something felt wrong inside her. Was the baby okay? She prayed to ask God what was wrong. God told her, "There are two children inside of you. They will become two nations."

God promised to give Abraham many children. He promised to make a special people out of Abraham's children. But God would not choose all of his children to be a part of this **special** people. God picked some men and women to be His own people. He picked some boys and girls. Now he told Isaac and Rebekah, "I will choose

one of your sons to be My people. The older will serve the younger."

Then Rebekah gave birth to twin boys. They were named Esau and Jacob. Their parents loved the boys and raised them in a godly home.

Esau was the oldest son. He became a skilled hunter. He loved to spend time outside hunting. But he didn't care about God. He despised the blessings God gave him.

One day Esau came home from hunting. He was very hungry. Jacob had made a pot of soup, and Esau wanted it. "Give me some soup!" he cried. "I'm starving!"

Jacob knew that Esau despised God. He knew Esau didn't care about God's blessings. Esau had a special blessing called a birthright. This blessing was for the oldest son in the family. But Esau didn't care about it. So Jacob said, "Give me your birthright, and I will give you some soup."

"What good is my birthright when I'm starving?" Esau cried. "You can have it! Just give me some food!" So he gave his birthright to Jacob. Then he ate the food and went away.

God blessed Jacob. He said, "I chose Jacob before he was born. I will make him and his children into My people. I will bless all nations in his children."

Then God told Jacob, "I am the Lord God. I am the God of Abraham. I am the God of Isaac your father. I promised to give them a land. I promised to make them My people. I will keep My promise with you. I have chosen you. I will be with you. I will keep you safe all your life."

Jacob was afraid. He said, "I am a sinful man. Can I live with God?" But he trusted God, too. He said, "The Lord will be my God." He trusted God's word. He had faith that God would keep His promise.

And the Lord said to her:
"Two nations are in your womb,
Two peoples shall be separated from your body;
One people shall be stronger than the other,
And the older shall serve the younger."
(Genesis 25:23)

Faith Lessons

God chooses sinful people — All people sin. God is holy. No sinful person can live with a holy God. But He chooses to save His people. He chooses sinful people and makes them His own. Praise God for this!

Esau despised God — Esau lived in a godly home. He had a godly mom and dad. But he didn't care. He despised these blessings. He despised God. We must not be like Esau. We must not despise what God gives us.

God will keep His promise — God promised to give Abraham a land. He promised to make his children into a mighty nation. God will keep His promise. But these people will still sin. So God also promised to send a Seed. That Seed will save His people from sin. God will keep this promise, too. He will send Jesus to save His people.

Jacob had faith in God — Jacob had faith in God and in His word. We must have faith in Him and His word, too.

Vocabulary

pregnant	parents	soup
special	about	birthright
younger	despise	

CHAPTER 11

Joseph Has Dreams

God blessed Jacob with many children. He had 12 sons. Some of his sons obeyed God, but some were wicked.

One son was named Joseph. Jacob loved Joseph very much. He gave him a special coat with many colors.

Joseph's brothers did not like him. They were angry that Jacob gave him a special coat. They did not love their brother like they should.

One night, Joseph had a dream. This was a special dream that came from God.

In the morning, Joseph told his brothers his dream. He said, "Please hear this dream I had. We were cutting wheat in the **field**, and we all had **bundles** of wheat. Then my **bundle** of wheat stood up, and your **bundles** of wheat bowed down to it."

Joseph's brothers got angry when they heard his dream. "Will you rule over us?" they said. "Do you think we'll bow down to you?"

Then Joseph had **another** dream. He was **surprised**. He

told his brothers and his father, "Look, I dreamed **another** dream. In this dream, the sun and moon and 11 stars bowed down to me."

Jacob was **surprised** to hear Joseph's dream, too. "Do you think your mother and I and your brothers will bow down to you?" he asked. Joseph's brothers got very angry, but Jacob didn't. He got very **quiet**. He didn't know why God sent these dreams, but he would wait to see what would happen. He trusted that God would do what was right.

The brothers didn't trust God. They hated Joseph and his dreams. They **decided** to kill Joseph. But one brother said, "Don't kill him!" So they **decided** to sell him as a slave.

The brothers took Joseph and sold him as a slave to men living far away. The men paid the brothers 20 **pieces** of silver. The brothers were happy to get the **money**. They watched as the men tied Joseph and took him away as a slave. Then they laughed and said, "Now what will happen to Joseph's dreams?"

The brothers took Joseph's coat. They killed a goat and dipped the coat in the goat's blood. "Now our father will think Joseph was killed by a wild beast," they said. So they took the coat to Jacob.

"We found this coat in the field," the brothers lied. They asked, "Is it Joseph's coat?"

Jacob took the coat. Then his eyes filled with tears. "Yes, it is Joseph's coat," he said. "My son has been killed by a wild animal!" Jacob cried and cried. He was very sad for many days. He didn't know the brothers had lied. He didn't know Joseph was still alive.

> *And he recognized it and said, "It is my son's tunic.*
> *A wild beast has devoured him.*
> *Without doubt Joseph is torn to pieces."*
> *(Genesis 37:33)*

Faith Lessons

God sees all things — Jacob didn't think Joseph was alive. He saw the coat and said, "He is dead." But God saw what happened to Joseph. He knew the brothers had lied. Nothing is hidden from God.

God has a plan — God had a plan to use Joseph. The brothers didn't understand this. Jacob and Joseph didn't understand it. But God would still make His plan happen.

We might not understand God's plan — Sometimes when bad things happen, we don't understand God's plan. But we must still trust Him. He made all things and rules all things, too. He has a very good plan. We can trust that He will do all things well.

Vocabulary

field	surprise	piece
bundle	quiet	money
another	decide	

CHAPTER 12

Joseph Is Faithful in Egypt

Joseph was led as a slave to Egypt. There a man bought him. The man told Joseph to work for him. Joseph obeyed. He did everything he could to help his new master. Joseph didn't want to be a slave, but he knew he must obey God and obey his master.

Joseph worked hard, and God blessed him. God blessed his master, too. Joseph's master was very glad to have Joseph as a slave. He made Joseph a ruler of all his land and everything he had. He trusted Joseph because Joseph obeyed God. Joseph was a righteous man. He obeyed God's Law and feared God, so Joseph's master knew he would do what was right.

But the master's wife was a wicked woman. She didn't want Joseph to obey God's Law. She wanted Joseph to sin. One day her husband was not home, so she said to Joseph, "Come sin with me."

But Joseph said, "No! I must obey God. I can't sin with you." Then he ran away from the woman.

This made the woman very angry, so she lied about Joseph. She told her husband that Joseph was a wicked man. Her husband sent Joseph to prison.

The prison was a dark, sad place. Joseph didn't want to be locked up there, but he couldn't get out. He was a slave, and he had to go where his master sent him.

Was Joseph sad in the prison? Would you be sad? Would you be angry?

Joseph said, "My brothers hate me. They sold me as a slave. Now my master's wife lied about me, so I am stuck in this prison." But Joseph wasn't angry. He trusted God. He said, "I didn't do anything wrong, and now I am a slave in prison. But I don't need to get angry. I will trust God. God is strong. He could have stopped my brothers if He wanted to. He could have stopped my master's wife from lying. But He didn't. This is part of His plan. I don't know what His plan is, but I will trust Him. He can **rescue** me from prison if He wants to. Or He can keep me in prison. I will trust Him, and I will obey Him no matter what happens."

Joseph was glad he could trust God. He wasn't afraid. He wasn't angry. He trusted God and followed Him.

The **guard** at the prison gave Joseph work to do. Joseph did his work **gladly**. He obeyed his new master, and God blessed him. The **guard** trusted Joseph and gave him important work to do. God was with Joseph and had mercy on him. Even in the prison, God was with him.

> *Then Joseph's master took him and put him into the prison,*
> *a place where the king's prisoners were confined.*
> *And he was there in the prison. But the LORD was*
> *with Joseph and showed him mercy.*
> *(Genesis 39:20-21)*

Faith Lessons

Joseph trusted God — Joseph didn't want to be a slave, but he trusted God. If God didn't want him to be a slave, God would set him free. Joseph trusted God and obeyed his master. He knew this would honor God. We must trust God even when things happen that we don't like. We must honor God even when it's hard.

Joseph didn't listen to sin — The master's wife wanted Joseph to sin. She asked him to sin with her. But Joseph didn't listen to her. He ran away from her. We must run away from sin, too. We must not listen when people ask us to sin.

God made all things — God made Joseph. He made Joseph's brothers. He made the wicked woman who lied about Joseph. God made all things and all people, and He rules over all. He can stop wicked people and wicked things. He will make everything work for His good plan. He will make all things work out for good for His people.

Vocabulary

Egypt	righteous	guard
bought	husband	gladly
ruler	rescue	

CHAPTER 13

Joseph Forgives His Brothers

Joseph lived as a slave in prison for a long time. Years passed. Two men were put in the prison. They served Pharaoh, the ruler of Egypt. The men had dreams, and Joseph told them what the dreams meant. God gave Joseph wisdom to understand the men's dreams.

Later, Pharaoh had a dream. He was worried by his dream. He didn't know what it meant, and none of his wise men could tell him what it meant. Then they called Joseph out of the prison and led him to Pharaoh. Pharaoh told Joseph his dream, and Joseph told him what it meant.

Joseph said, "God sent this dream to tell you what will happen. There will be seven years of good harvest in Egypt.

The land will **grow** lots and lots of food. But then seven years of **famine** will come. No food will **grow**, and all your people will have nothing to eat. You must save food **during** the good years. If you don't, all of Egypt will starve when the **famine** comes."

Joseph told **Pharaoh**, "Find a man you can trust. Let him gather food **during** the good years. Then all your people will

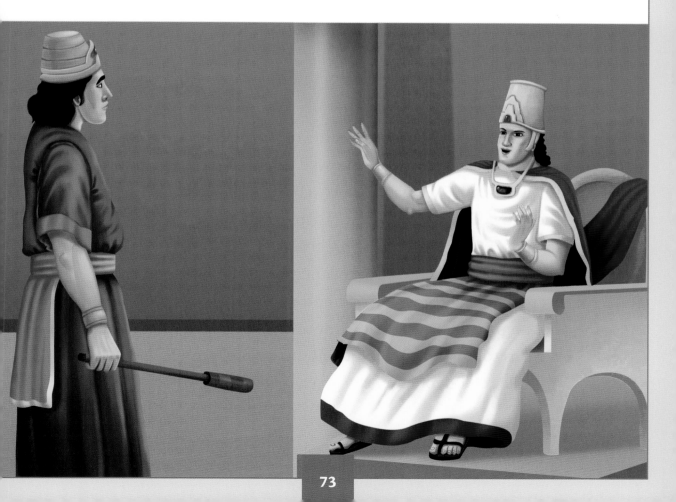

have food to eat in the **famine**."

Pharaoh said, "You are a wise man, and God is with you. I will make you ruler over all Egypt. You will prepare my nation for the **famine**." **Pharaoh** gave Joseph his ring and a special robe. Joseph was surprised. **Suddenly** he wasn't in prison anymore. Now he was ruler over all of Egypt!

Joseph worked hard to get Egypt ready for the **famine**. He stored up lots of food in large store houses. When the **famine** came, all the people had food to eat.

But in Canaan, the people didn't have anything to eat. Jacob and his sons ran out of food, so Jacob sent his sons to Egypt to buy some food.

When Joseph's brothers came to Egypt, Joseph saw them. The brothers came up and bowed to him. They didn't know it was Joseph. "We have come to buy food," they said as they bowed down to Joseph. Then Joseph remembered his dreams. His dreams had come true.

Joseph said, "I am your brother Joseph." His brothers were very **frightened**, but Joseph said, "Don't be afraid. I'm not angry at you. You hated me and sold me as a slave. You did this to hurt me, but God did this to keep us safe. Now I am ruler of Egypt and I can give you food. Now you won't starve in the **famine**. This was God's plan. He sent me to Egypt as a slave so that we could all stay alive."

Joseph's brothers went back to Canaan. They told Jacob, "Joseph is still alive!" Jacob was so surprised that he didn't believe them. "Can he be alive?" he asked. Then he was filled with joy. "I will go see my son!" he cried.

Jacob and all his family came to Egypt. Joseph was glad to see them and gave them a place to live. He gave them food for the **famine**. Now none of his family would starve.

God had planned a **wonderful** plan. He made Joseph become a slave and sent him to prison so that he could keep his family alive. God made all things happen for good. Very bad things happened, but God used these things to bring good to His people. Now His people were safe in Egypt, and they would not starve in the **famine**. God is a very wise and merciful God!

"But as for you, you meant evil against me; but God meant it for good, in order to bring it about as it is this day, to save many people alive."
(Genesis 50:20)

Faith Lessons

Joseph forgave his brothers — Joseph's brothers sinned and did very bad things. But Joseph didn't get angry at them. He forgave his brothers. He loved them and gave them food even after they sold him as a slave. We must forgive like Joseph.

God is a wise God — Joseph didn't know why he was a slave. He didn't know why he was in prison. But God knew. He had a plan to save Joseph's family from the famine. He is a very wise God.

Joseph is a picture of Jesus — We are all like Joseph's brothers. We sin and we hate what is good. But Jesus came to save us from sin. He loved us even when we hated Him. He is a very good God. Let us praise Him!

Vocabulary

Pharaoh	famine	frighten
meant	during	wonderful
grow	suddenly	

CHAPTER 14

Israel Cries Out to God for Help

Jacob and his family lived in Egypt for many years. Jacob grew old and died. Then his sons grew old and died. But his family kept growing. It grew and grew. God blessed his family with many children. They were called the children of Israel. Soon there were thousands and thousands of them. They lived together in Egypt.

Pharaoh was the ruler of Egypt. He was afraid of the children of Israel. He said, "The people of Israel are increasing. Soon they will be stronger and mightier than we are! We must stop them from growing. We must find a way to make them weaker than we are."

Pharaoh made all the people of Israel slaves. He forced

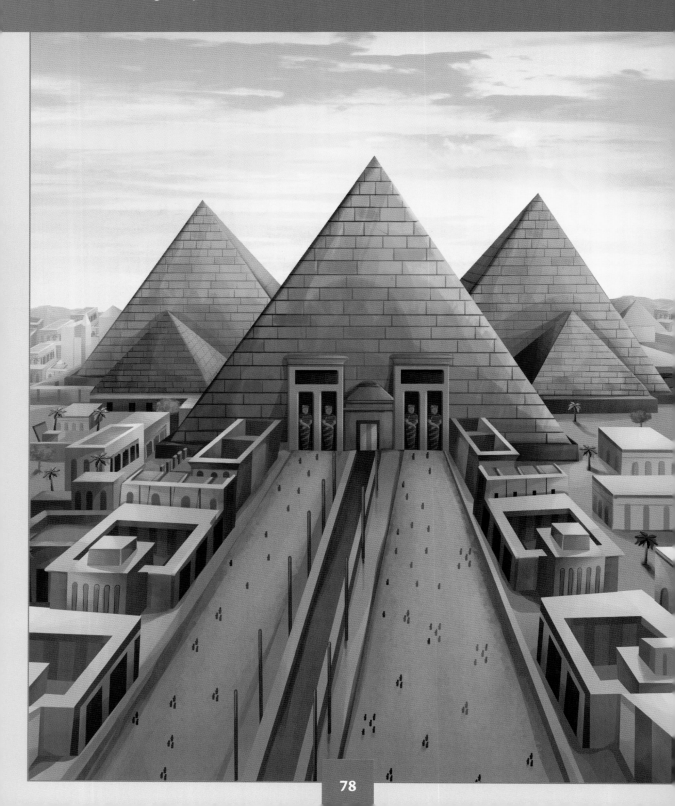

them to work hard to build cities for him. He made their lives very **difficult**. He sent harsh masters to rule over them. The masters made them work very, very hard. They treated them badly. The people of **Israel** didn't like the hard work. They didn't like being slaves. They were sad and groaned because of their hard life. It was a very unhappy time for them.

The people couldn't escape from Pharaoh. They were stuck being slaves. So they prayed to God. They cried to the Lord and asked Him to **deliver** them.

God heard the cry of the children of **Israel**. He saw their **difficult** lives. He saw the hard work Pharaoh made them do. Then He said, "I remember My covenant. I made a promise to Abraham. I promised to bless him with many children. I told him that wicked men would want to hurt his children. But I promised to keep his children safe."

God said, "I promised to give him a land. Now I will keep My promise. I will save his children from slavery in Egypt. I will bring them out and give them the land I promised them."

God said, "I made a covenant with Isaac, too. And I made a covenant with Jacob. I have not forgotten My covenant.

Now I will keep My promise to their children. I will rescue them from Egypt. I will be their God, and they will be My people."

Then the children of Israel groaned because of the bondage, and they cried out; and their cry came up to God because of the bondage. So God heard their groaning, and God remembered His covenant with Abraham, with Isaac, and with Jacob.
(Exodus 2:23-24)

Faith Lessons

The children of Israel cried to God — The people were slaves. They had to work very hard. Their life was very difficult. So they cried to God. They knew He would hear their prayer. We can pray to God, too. God always hears His people pray.

God remembered His covenant — Abraham had died a long time ago. But God did not forget His promise to him. He never forgets. He will always keep His promises. We can trust Him just like Abraham did.

Vocabulary

Israel	mightier	difficult
increasing	force	deliver

CHAPTER 15

God Protects Moses

The king of Egypt did not like Israel. He didn't want the **children** of Israel to grow stronger, so he made a plan. It was a very wicked plan. He told his people, "Kill all the baby boys that are born to the people of Israel." He told them to throw the babies into the river.

One mother had a little baby boy. She knew the king wanted to kill the baby, so she hid him. She made a little basket for her son and put him inside it. Then she hid the basket in some tall **reeds** growing beside the river. Her daughter watched the basket to keep the baby safe.

But suddenly a woman came to the river. She was the daughter of Pharaoh. She was a **princess** in Egypt. When she got to the river, she saw the little basket in the **reeds**. She called her servant and said, "Bring me that basket." The servant **brought** it, and the **princess** opened the basket. Inside she saw the little baby boy, and the baby started to cry.

The **princess** felt sorry for the little boy. "This is one of the babies from Israel," she said. She knew her father wanted to kill the **child**, but she decided to keep the baby. "I will

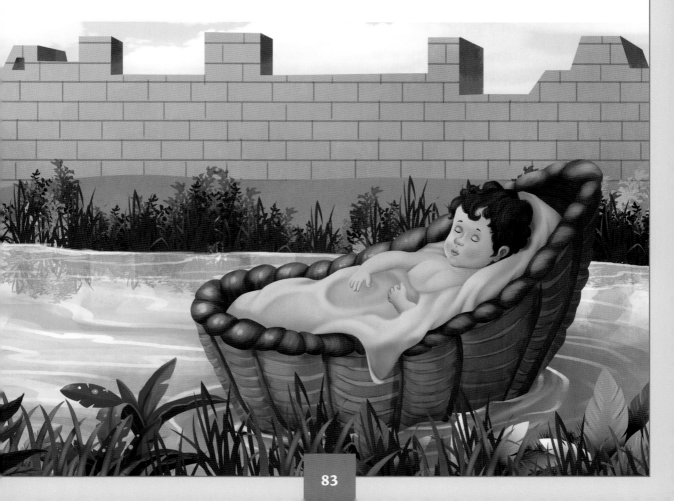

keep him safe," she said. "I will raise him as my son." Then she named him Moses.

Moses grew up in Egypt with the princess, but he wasn't an Egyptian. He was an Israelite. Israelite is what the people of Israel were called. When Moses became a man, he left Pharaoh's home. He knew he belonged with the people of Israel. These people were God's people, and Moses wanted to follow God. He didn't want to follow the wicked ways of Egypt.

Moses left Egypt and went to another country. He met a man named Jethro and married his daughter. Then God blessed Moses and gave him two sons.

One day God said to Moses, "I am your God. I am the God of My people Israel. I hear My people praying to Me. I hear them groaning because of the wicked things the king is doing to them. I have chosen you. I will use you to bring My people out of Egypt. I will save them from the king and will bring them to the land I promised them."

Moses was scared when God told him this. He was afraid to go to the king of Egypt. He was afraid the king would kill him. He was also afraid that the Israelites wouldn't listen to him.

But God said, "I will be with you."

Moses knew that God was strong. He could keep Moses safe. He could rescue the people of Israel from Pharaoh. He would keep His promises. So Moses trusted God.

But Moses said to God, "Who am I that I should go to Pharaoh, and that I should bring the children of Israel out of Egypt?" So He said, "I will certainly be with you."
(Exodus 3:11-12)

Faith Lessons

Satan hates God's people — Satan hates God. He hates God's people, too. He will always try to destroy them. Pharaoh tried to kill all the boy babies in Israel. This was Satan's plan. But God didn't let his plan work. God protected His people. He will always protect His people. Satan will never win.

God is Lord over everything — God made everything. He made the river in Egypt. And He made the weeds growing by the river. He made Moses and Moses' mother. He is Lord over all things He made. He kept Moses safe in the basket by the river. Then He brought the princess to the river to find Moses. He is Lord over all, and He rules the whole world.

God kept His promise — God made a promise to save His people. Now He would keep His promise. He heard their prayers. He saw their pain. And He prepared a way to set them free. He is a very good God. Let us praise Him!

Vocabulary

reed	child	Israelite
princess	children	belonged
brought	Egyptian	scared

CHAPTER 16

Pharaoh Will Not Fear God

Moses went to the king of Egypt. He said to him, "The Lord God of Israel says, 'Let My people go.'"

But Pharaoh didn't believe in the true God. He didn't think God was strong **enough** to save His people. "Who is this God?" he asked. "Why should I obey His voice and let the people of Israel go? I will not obey this God, and I will not let Israel go!"

Then God told Moses, "I will show Pharaoh that I am the Lord. I will show him My power. I will stretch out My hand over Egypt and will do amazing **wonders** in the land. Then he will let you go."

God sent **terrible plagues** on Egypt. He turned the water of the river into blood. Then he sent frogs and lice and flies. He stretched out His hand over all the cattle and flocks of sheep and killed them. Then He sent a sickness on the people. He sent fire and hail to destroy their crops and their fields. Locusts came and ate anything that was left.

Soon the land of Egypt was destroyed. The people were sick, their food was gone, and their cows and sheep were dead. But still Pharaoh **refused** to let the people of Israel go free.

Then God said, "I will send one more **plague** on Egypt. Because they will not let My people go, I will kill their firstborn sons. In every home in Egypt, I will kill the oldest son. But I will keep the sons of My people safe."

God told Moses, "Tell every family in Israel to take a lamb from their flocks. It must be a lamb with nothing wrong with it. Tell them to kill the lamb and put some of its blood around their doors. Then they must go inside their houses and eat the lamb."

Then God **explained**, "Tonight I will pass **through** the land of Egypt. I will strike and kill all the firstborn in the land. But when I see the blood on your doors, I will pass over you and will not kill you. This is My **Passover**. This is a special feast that you must keep every year to remember what I will do for you."

Moses called the leaders of Israel. He told them what God had said. The people were very glad to hear this. They worshiped God and thanked Him for His promise to deliver them. Then all the people took a lamb and killed it. They put the blood on the sides of their door just like God told them to. When they finished, they went inside and ate the lamb.

Then the sun set. Darkness covered the land. All was quiet in Egypt. But at midnight God struck all the firstborn sons. He killed every one of them. In every home **through** all the land of Egypt, someone died. But in the homes where the blood was on the doorposts, God passed over the house and didn't kill anyone.

And it shall be, when your children say to you, "What do you mean by this service?" that you shall say, "It is the Passover sacrifice of the LORD, who passed over the houses of the children of Israel in Egypt when He struck the Egyptians and delivered our households."
(Exodus 12:26-27)

Faith Lessons

Pharaoh didn't believe God — God told Pharaoh to let the people of Israel go. But the king didn't believe that God was strong or powerful. He trusted in his own strength and in his false gods. We must not be like Pharaoh. We must never trust in anything except God.

God rules over all — The king of Egypt didn't fear God, so God sent plagues on the land. He showed His power to Egypt. Then the people were afraid. They knew that the Lord is the only true God. He rules over all things. All the world is in His hand.

Passover is a picture of Jesus saving us — The blood on the doorposts saved the people inside the house. God saw the blood and didn't kill them. This is a picture of what Jesus did. He died to save His people. Now God looks at Jesus and sees the sacrifice He made. This is why His people are saved. They are covered by the blood of Jesus.

Vocabulary

enough	plague	through
wonders	refuse	Passover
terrible	explain	

CHAPTER 17

God Opens the Red Sea

When God killed the firstborn in Egypt, Pharaoh and his people were afraid. They were **terrified** of the power of God. They called Moses and said, "Get out! Take the people of Israel and go away!"

Moses called the Israelites together and they left Egypt. The people were filled with joy as they left. They **weren't** slaves anymore! They were free!

God led the people into the **wilderness**. This was a desert place. God told the people, "I will be your God and you will be My people. Follow Me and walk in My ways."

The people were glad to have the Lord as their God. He was a powerful God. He had judged Egypt and set them free. But would the people trust God? They **weren't** slaves now. They were free! But would they still act like slaves? Or would they act like free men who trusted God?

The people didn't know which way to go, so God led them. He sent a **pillar** of clouds in front of them to show them the way. At night, He sent a **pillar** of fire. Now they knew where to go. They followed the cloud and the fire.

God led the people to the Red Sea. Mountains stood on **either** side of them. They couldn't get around the sea, and they couldn't get across it. What would they do now? They didn't know what to do, but God knew. He had a plan.

Just then, someone started shouting. "The Egyptians are coming! Pharaoh and his chariots are chasing us!" The people of Israel looked behind them. They could see the army of Egypt racing toward them.

"They will kill us all!" they cried. "Why did we leave Egypt? Now we will die here! Who can save us?"

The people cried out in fear, but Moses said to them, "Don't be afraid! God will save us! Don't you remember what He did in Egypt? Trust Him. He will save us. Stand still and watch, and you will see the **salvation** of the Lord."

God told Moses, "Today I will gain **honor** over Pharaoh

and his army. Then all people will know that I am the Lord."

Then God sent a strong, strong wind. It blew on the Red Sea and moved the waters out of the way. Soon dry land appeared in the sea. The people of Israel crossed through the sea on the dry land, and the water stood up like walls beside them. They crossed the sea in **safety** and made it to the other side.

Pharaoh and his army tried to cross through the sea, too. But God sent the waters crashing back down over them, and they were all destroyed. The people of Israel looked back and saw the dead bodies of the Egyptians lying on the shore. God had delivered them again! He had sent His **salvation** and saved them from their enemies!

And Moses said to the people, "Do not be afraid. Stand still, and see the salvation of the LORD, which He will accomplish for you today. For the Egyptians whom you see today, you shall see again no more forever."

(Exodus 14:13)

Faith Lessons

The people of Israel were free, but they acted like slaves — God saved the people from Egypt. He set them free. But the people didn't act like free people. They acted like slaves. They were still afraid of their old masters in Egypt. They didn't trust God.

God had a plan — God led His people to the Red Sea. He did this to show His power to His people and to judge Egypt. This brought glory to God. The people saw His power and honored Him.

We can trust God — The people of Israel were afraid, but God was not afraid. He rules all things, and He will make all things good. We should not be like the people of Israel. We must not be afraid of people. We must fear the Lord and trust Him.

Vocabulary

terrified	pillar	honor
weren't	either	safety
wilderness	salvation	

CHAPTER 18

God Gives Manna

The Israelites were very glad that God saved them from Pharaoh and the army of Egypt. Now their enemies were dead, and the people **rejoiced**. They sang a song of praise to God. They sang,

"Who is like You, O Lord?
You are glorious in holiness.
You do mighty wonders.
You stretched out Your right hand
And saved Your people.
The Lord shall reign forever and ever!"

God heard the people sing praise to Him. Then He said,

"If you are careful to listen to Me and to do what is right, I will protect you and keep you safe. You must obey My **commandments** and listen to My laws. Then I will not punish you with the plagues I sent on Egypt. For I am the Lord who heals you."

God led the people through the wilderness. But the people began to get **worried**. Where would they find food in the desert? Soon they started to **complain**. "We should have stayed in Egypt!" they cried. "We would still be slaves, but at least we would have food to eat!"

Then the people got angry at Moses. "Why did you bring us out of Egypt?" they **complained**. "We wanted to stay there!"

The people of Israel were wrong to get angry. They sinned **against** God by **complaining**. But God had mercy on them. He said, "I will rain down **bread** from heaven for you. I will feed you in the desert."

Did the people believe God? Could He really send **bread** from heaven? That night all the people of Israel went to bed in their tents. When they woke up in the morning, something **strange** was on the ground. It was small and white. "What is it?" they asked.

Moses said, "This is the food God sent for you." The people picked it up and tasted it. It tasted very good! They liked it. "It tastes like **bread** with honey," they said.

Each person gathered as much as he needed. On the next morning, God sent more **bread** from heaven. Every day He sent enough for all the people to eat. They called this special food manna.

"Who is like You, O LORD, among the gods?
Who is like You, glorious in holiness,
Fearful in praises, doing wonders?"
(Exodus 15:11)

Faith Lessons

The people forgot who God was — The Israelites sang praises to God for saving them from the Egyptians. But then they forgot Him and complained about food. They didn't trust God, and they forgot what He had done for them. This was sin. We must not forget what God has done for us. Let us always remember, and let us always praise Him.

The people were angry at God — The people got mad at Moses for leading them out of Egypt into the desert. But they weren't really mad at Moses. They were mad at God. God was the One who led them into the desert. When we complain, we are telling God that He is not good enough for us. We are telling Him that what He gives us is not good. This is sin.

God has mercy on sinful people — The Israelites sinned very much. They didn't trust God. They complained about Him. They wanted to go back to Egypt. But God still had mercy on them. He is a very merciful God. Let us thank Him for His mercy and His grace!

Vocabulary

rejoice	commandment	against
glorious	worried	bread
reign	complain	strange

CHAPTER 19

Jethro Gives Good Advice

The people of Israel lived in the desert. They followed where God led them. Jethro, the father of Moses' wife, heard what God had done for Israel. He heard that God had rescued Israel and saved them from Egypt. So Jethro came to see Moses and to hear about the things God had done.

Moses was glad to see Jethro. He told him everything God had done for His people. Jethro was filled with joy to hear about the mighty works of God. He said, "**Blessed** be the Lord who has delivered you from Pharaoh! Now I know that the Lord is greater than all false gods."

The next morning, Moses got up to talk with the people

of Israel. **Whenever** someone had a problem, they came to
Moses for an **answer**. Moses would tell them what the right
thing to do was. If two people **argued**, they would come
to Moses and tell him the **argument**. Then Moses would
tell them who was right and who was wrong. He explained
God's Law to the people. God's Law told the people what
God was like. It also **taught** them how they should live.

Moses sat down, and the people came to him. They started coming in the morning, and they came all the way until the evening. A long, long line of people stood in front of Moses' tent. They were all waiting to talk to him and hear what he would tell them.

Jethro watched this. Then he said to Moses, "This is not good. You will get very tired trying to help all these people. And the people will get very tired waiting for you to help them. You can't teach these people all by **yourself**. You need help."

Jethro said, "This is what you should do. Find wise men. Find men who fear God and who tell the truth, and let them help you. You can make them rulers over small **groups** of people. They will teach the people God's Law and will show the people what is right. Then, if they can't find an **answer** to something, they can come to you and you can help them. This way you won't get tired. And the people won't get tired, either. These wise men can be judges for the people. Then things will be **easier** for all of you."

Moses listened to what Jethro told him. He said, "This is very wise. I will do what you say." Moses found many wise men in Israel. He found men who feared God and who told the truth. He found men who weren't greedy and who knew God's Law. Then he made these men judges over the people. When the people had a problem, they went to these wise judges. The men **taught** the people God's Law. Now it was much **easier** for Moses, and it was much **easier** for the people, too.

> *"You shall select from all the people able men, such as fear God, men of truth, hating covetousness; . . . So it will be easier for you, for they will bear the burden with you."*
> *(Exodus 18:21-22)*

Faith Lessons

Jethro praised God for His goodness — Jethro was not part of Israel. He belonged to a different nation. But he still praised God for His goodness. God said that He would choose people from all nations to be His people. He chose people like Jethro even though they were not from Israel. God is a very good and merciful God.

Moses listened to Jethro — Moses was a wise man, but he still listened to Jethro. Jethro was older than Moses. Moses honored him and listened to what he said. It is good to honor those who are older than we are.

God loves His people and gives them rulers — Sin makes us blind. Because of sin, we can't tell what is right and wrong. God is very merciful to us. He gives us rulers and pastors. He wants these men to teach us what is right and wrong.

Rulers should be wise men who fear God — Wicked men don't understand God's Law. They won't know what is good and right. So God tells us to choose wise men for our rulers. He tells us to choose men who fear God and who tell the truth. God's ways are very good for us.

Vocabulary

blessed	argue	yourself
whenever	argument	group
answer	taught	easier

CHAPTER 20

The Ten Commandments

God led the Israelites to a mountain called **Sinai**. He had something very special to give to His people, and He would give it to them on this mountain.

God told the people, "You saw what I did to the Egyptians. You were slaves, but I came and rescued you. I picked you up and carried you away just like an **eagle** picks up its little chicks and carries them. I saved you from your enemies and kept you safe, and I have brought you to Myself. Now, if you will obey Me and keep My covenant, then you will be My special **treasure** in the world. All the earth is Mine, but you will be Mine in a very special way. This is the covenant I make with you and with your children."

Then God spoke to the people from the mountain. He gave them ten laws. These are the laws of God. He said:

1. "I am your God. Do not worship any other god. Trust in Me, and do not trust in other gods."

2. "Do not make a picture of Me. Do not worship any other thing. You must worship Me in the way I tell you. Do not worship Me any other way."

3. "**Respect** My name. Do not make fun of My name or use it in a silly way."

4. "Remember the Sabbath day. Don't work on this day, but rest on it and keep it holy."

5. "Honor your father and mother."

6. "Do not kill a person. Protect the life of other people."

7. "Husbands and wives make a promise when they **marry**. Do not **break** this promise. You must keep it."

8. "Do not steal."

9. "Do not lie."

10. "Be glad for what you have. Don't want something that other people have. Don't wish that it was yours."

The people heard the Lord speak from the mountain. They were terrified to hear God speak. They said to Moses, "You speak with us, but don't let God speak to us or we'll die!"

But Moses said, "Don't be afraid. God has come to test you. He has come to put His fear on you so that you won't sin."

The people stood very far away from the mountain because they were afraid of God. Would they trust Him now? Would they obey His Law? We must wait and see.

"You have seen what I did to the Egyptians, and how I bore you on eagles' wings and brought you to Myself. Now therefore, if you will indeed obey My voice and keep My covenant, then you shall be a special treasure to Me above all people; for all the earth is Mine."
(Exodus 19:4-5)

Faith Lessons

God rules the world in a good way — God made the world, so He knows how to make it work properly. If a man makes a toy, he knows how the toy should work. God is the same way. He tells us how the world works when He gives us His Law. It is a good law, and it is good for us and for our world.

Sin makes us foolish — God gave His Law to Adam, but Adam sinned and forgot God's Law. We forget it too because of our sin. God has pity on His people and wrote His Law down so that they could remember it forever. He is a very merciful and loving God. Let us thank Him for His Law.

Jesus is the only One who can save from sin — We sin every day. God's Law teaches us what sin is. But His Law can't make us good. It can't save us from our sin. Only Jesus can do that. We must pray to Him and ask Him to save us from our sin.

Vocabulary

Sinai	respect	properly
eagle	marry	
treasure	break	

CHAPTER 21

God Gives a Good Law

God made the world very good, but then Adam and Eve sinned. Now the world is broken because of sin. Now all the world isn't very good like God made it. Bad things are in the world, and bad things happen in the world. This happens because of sin.

God loves the world He made. It makes Him very sad to see it full of sin. The people He made do very wicked things. This makes God sad, too. He sees the people He made, and He has **compassion** on them. **Compassion** means He has pity on them and wants to help them. Even though people sin, God still has mercy on them. This is why He gave us His Law.

God saved the Israelites from Egypt when they were

slaves. The Egyptians treated His people with **cruelty**. Egypt did very wicked things to them and tried to kill their baby boys. God rescued the Israelites and brought them out of Egypt to make them free. But the people weren't free from sin. They had wicked sin in their hearts just like the people of Egypt did.

Now the people lived in the desert. They didn't have houses to live in here, so they lived in tents. Sometimes they got angry and said mean things to each other. Sometimes they did wicked things and started fighting with each other. They were mean to each other just like the Egyptians had been mean to them.

God said, "My world is broken because of sin. Now people do bad things and hurt each other. I have pity on the people and don't want them to hurt each other. I will give My people My Law. I want them to be holy like I am holy. I want them to love like I love."

God told the people, "I will give you My Law, and you must obey it. You must not hate your brother in your heart. You must love your **neighbor** as yourself."

God told His people to love one **another**. Love is a picture of what God is like.

When the people of Israel were slaves in Egypt, they had no one to help them. They were like little children who have no father or mother to protect them. But God protected them. He said, "I will be a Father to you, and you will be My children." God is a very loving God!

God wants His people to love like He loves. Some people in Israel needed help. Some women got married, but then their husbands died. These women were called widows. They had no one to care for them. Some children had lost their parents. Their parents had died, and now the children were orphans. They had no one to care for them. But God cared about them. He wanted His people to care, too. He told them to take care of widows and orphans. This was part of His Law.

When Israel left Egypt, some Egyptians came with them. The Egyptians wanted to stay with Israel because they were God's people. Now these families from Egypt were a long way from home. They were strangers, and the people of Israel might not be nice to them. But God told them to love the strangers. This was part of His Law, too.

God told His people, "Don't treat a stranger badly. Don't be mean to any widow or orphan. If you are mean to them,

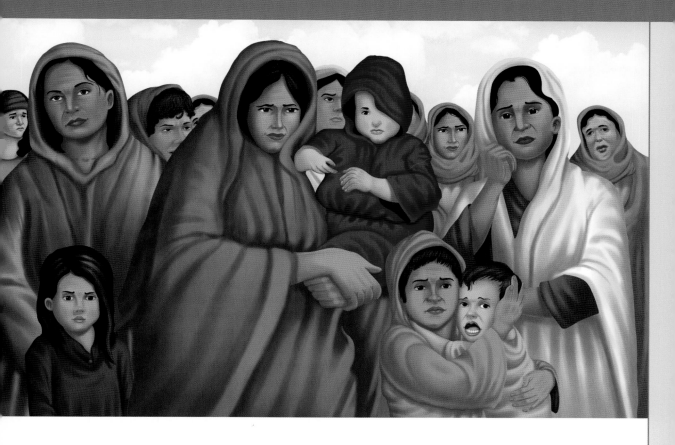

they will cry out to Me for help, and I will hear their cry. I watch over the strangers. I help the orphans and widows, but I will destroy the wicked."

God loves His world, and He hates sin. He is a very good God. He is a compassionate God. He loves His world and the people He made, and He wants us to love them, too.

As a father pities his children,
*So the L*ORD *pities those who fear Him.*
(Psalm 103:13)

Faith Lessons

The world is broken because of sin — God made all things good, but sin brings evil into the world. One day God will judge the world for sin. Then He will make all things new, and His world will be very good again.

God is a Father who takes care of His children — All people sin, but God still takes care of the world He created. He is a very good and merciful God. He is like a Father to His children.

God gave us a good law — God's Law is very good. His Law cannot save us from sin, but it tells us what God is like. It is good for us to study His Law. It is good for all people and all nations to obey it.

Vocabulary

compassion   another   stranger
cruelty   widow
neighbor   orphan

CHAPTER 22

Spies Are Sent into Canaan

God promised to give a land to Abraham. Now He led the people of Israel to this land. This was the land of Canaan. The land was filled with wicked people, and the Israelites had to fight these people to take the land. But God promised to be with His people and fight for them.

God told Moses, "Choose twelve men from the people of Israel. Tell them to go into the land of Canaan and look at the land. They will see what the land is like. Then I will lead you into the land and give it to you like I promised."

Moses chose twelve men and sent them into Canaan. He told them, "Go see what the land is like. See what the people are like. We must fight them, so we need to know if they have strong cities. But don't be afraid. Be full of **courage**, for God is with you."

The **twelve** men went into the land and looked around. It was a very good place to live. It had good food and good land in it. But the people in the land were very strong. They had strong cities to protect them.

When the **twelve** men came back to Israel, they brought some fruit from Canaan. They brought a **cluster** of grapes that was so big it took two men to carry it! Then ten of the men told the people, "The land is a very good land. There is **plenty** of good food there. We would like to live there. But the people are very strong! We will never be able to fight against them and win. They are so big that we look like **grasshoppers** beside them!"

The people were scared when they heard this. But two of the **twelve** men said, "Don't be afraid! The people are strong, and they have strong cities. But we don't need to fear them. Our God will fight for us. We must trust Him and have **courage**!" These two men were Joshua and Caleb.

But the people didn't believe Joshua and Caleb. They believed the other ten men. They said, "We can't fight

against the people in Canaan. They would kill us! We must not go into the land! We should have stayed in Egypt! Now we will all die!" The people were so scared that they started to cry.

Joshua and Caleb said, "Don't cry! God will fight for us. We don't need to be afraid."

But the people didn't believe them. They got angry and said, "Let's kill Joshua and Caleb!"

God heard what the people said. He said, "How long will this people reject Me? I promised to give them the land, but they won't believe Me. Now I will punish them for their sin."

God sent a sickness on the ten men who went into the land and were afraid. These ten men all died because they didn't believe God. But Joshua and Caleb didn't die.

Then God said to the people of Israel, "I promised to give you the land of Canaan. It is a very good land. But you sinned. You didn't trust Me. You are afraid of the people of Canaan, so I will not give you the land. You will spend the rest of your lives in the desert, and you will die there. Then, after you are dead, I will bring your children into the land I promised."

God told the people, "I have spoken this, and I will do it.

You will all die in the desert. But Joshua and Caleb will not die. They trusted Me, and I will keep them safe. They will go into the good land I promised them. They and their children will live in the land."

> "I the LORD have spoken this. I will surely do so to all this
> evil congregation who are gathered together against Me.
> In this wilderness they shall be consumed,
> and there they shall die."
> (Numbers 14:35)

Faith Lessons

God is a strong God — Israel was afraid of the people of Canaan, but God was stronger than all the people. He could defeat the people in Canaan. He is a very strong God. No one is able to fight against Him. We must not fear people. We should fear and obey God.

God judged the people — Israel didn't believe God was strong enough to save them. The ten men told them not to trust God. This was a terrible sin, and God judged the ten men and the people of Israel for this sin. He killed them all.

Joshua and Caleb believed God — They trusted that God would keep His promise. God was very pleased with them. He wants us to trust Him. He tells us to trust Him in His Word. We must believe Him just like Joshua and Caleb did.

Vocabulary

twelve	plenty	defeat
courage	grasshopper	
cluster	reject	

CHAPTER 23

Rahab Saves the Spies

For forty years the people of Israel lived in the wilderness. All the older people died. Then God told Moses, "It's time for the people to go live in the land I gave them. But tell them that they must obey Me. They must obey My Law and trust Me."

Then God said, "I know these people will not obey Me. They will turn away from Me and will do very wicked things. Then I will become angry and will punish them."

Moses called the people together. He told them, "God is perfect. He is full of justice. But you are foolish and unwise. Why don't you trust God? He is your Father, isn't He? He bought you and saved you. You must not forget what He has done for you. You must remember and must turn from your sins. Then He will forgive you and save you."

Moses was very old. He spoke these words to Israel, and then he died.

After Moses died, God told Joshua, "I have chosen you to lead the people into the land I promised them. Don't be afraid. Trust in Me and be full of courage."

Joshua prepared to fight the first city in the land. It was called **Jericho**. He sent two men to spy on the city and see what it was like.

The men went to the city and went inside the gates. They came to a house in the city. A woman named Rahab lived there. But the king of the city **discovered** that the men of Israel had come. He **searched** through the city to find them and kill them.

Rahab heard that the king was looking for the men. She told them, "The king wants to kill you! **Quickly**, come up to my roof, and I will hide you!"

Rahab hid the men until the king's soldiers had left. But now it was night and the city gates were shut. The men couldn't get out of the city. But Rahab's house was part of the city's walls. She had a window in her house, so she tied a rope

in the window and let the men escape out her window. She told them, "Go hide in the mountains until the soldiers stop searching for you. Then you can go back to Israel in safety."

Rahab knew that God would fight for Israel and would defeat Jericho. She said to the men, "I know that your God is strong. He will give you the land. But please remember me when you come to fight my city. Please don't kill me, and please don't kill my family."

The men were very grateful to Rahab. They said, "You saved our lives. You protected us when the king's soldiers wanted to kill us. Now we will protect you. When we come to destroy your city, we won't kill you or your family. We will remember your kindness."

Then the men escaped into the darkness and went to the mountains to hide. Rahab watched them go. She knew they would come back and destroy her city. They would kill everyone, but she trusted that they would remember their promise. She trusted they would keep her and her family safe.

[Rahab said] "The Lord your God, He is God in heaven above and on earth beneath. Now therefore, I beg you, swear to me by the Lord, since I have shown you kindness, that you also will show kindness to my father's house."
(Joshua 2:11-12)

Faith Lessons

God knows all things — God knew that the people of Israel would forget Him. He knew they would disobey Him and do wicked things. He knows all things. Nothing is hidden from Him.

We are sinful — We are like Israel. We can't obey God's Law. We don't love God like He tells us to. We are selfish and have sinful hearts. We need God to change our heart so that we can love Him and obey Him. He sent Jesus Christ to do this.

God can save — Rahab was a sinful woman, but she trusted God. She knew He was strong enough to save her from death. We must trust God, too. He is strong enough to save us from sin and death.

Vocabulary

justice	discover	grateful
unwise	search	kindness
Jericho	quickly	

CHAPTER 24

God Fights Against Jericho

I t was time for Israel to go into the land God promised them. But first they had to cross a deep river. This river was called Jordan. It was a strong, rushing river. Its waters were filled with **danger**. The people didn't know how to get across the river. They didn't know what to do, but God said He would make a way.

When the people reached the river, God pushed all the water back. It piled up into a big heap! Then the people crossed through the **riverbed** on dry ground. Now they were in the land of Canaan! This was the land God promised them!

After the people crossed the river, God said, "Send twelve men back into the river. Tell them to gather big stones out of the **riverbed**. Then I want you to set these stones up in the new land I give you. These stones will be a **memorial** for you. They will help you remember what I have done for you. When you see these stones, you will **recall** that I pushed the waters of the Jordan River out of your way so that you could cross over on dry ground."

The twelve men obeyed God. They went back into the

river. Then they gathered big stones and made a **memorial** for the people. God told them, "Your children won't know what these stones mean. They will ask you, 'Why is there a big pile of stones here? Who put these here? What do they mean?' Then you must tell them what I did for you. You must teach your children about Me. You must teach them about My works. These stones will be a **useful reminder**. They will **remind** you of what I did and who I am."

Now it was time to **attack** Jericho. God told Joshua, "You won't need to fight this city. I will fight for you." God did just what He said. He told the people to march around the city. Then God broke down all the walls. Joshua and his army rushed into the city to kill the people there and take the city.

But Joshua didn't forget Rahab. He called the two men who went to spy on Jericho. He told them, "Run to Rahab's house. Find her. Find her family. Then take them to safety. We don't want them to get hurt in the battle." The men ran to Rahab's house. They took her and her family and led them out of the city so they would be safe.

After the battle, Rahab and her family lived with the people of Israel. Rahab was very glad to live there. She married one of the men from Israel. She became part of God's people.

She trusted God, and she wanted to live with His people and worship Him. God protected her from her enemies and saved her life. Rahab would always remember that He saved her and her family from death.

> *And Joshua spared Rahab the harlot, her father's household,*
> *and all that she had. So she dwells in Israel to this day,*
> *because she hid the messengers whom*
> *Joshua sent to spy out Jericho.*
> *(Joshua 6:25)*

Faith Lessons

God wants us to remember — God led His people through the Jordan River just like He led them through the Red Sea. He wanted His people to remember that He protected them. That's why He told them to set up a pile of stones. We must be like the Israelites. We must remember what God has done for us. He has done many good things for us. It's good to talk about these things. It's good to thank Him for them.

God chooses people from all nations — Rahab was not an Israelite, but God chose her to be part of His special people. He chooses people from all nations to be His own people. Let us praise Him for this!

Vocabulary

danger	recall	attack
riverbed	useful	
memorial	reminder	

CHAPTER 25

God Makes Gideon Brave

Now Israel lived in the land God gave them. God fought for them and killed their enemies. But the people didn't obey God. After Joshua got old and died, the people stopped trusting God. They started worshiping the gods of Canaan.

God saw what His people did, so He punished them. He sent an enemy nation to fight them. The nation was called Midian. They stole the people's food and things. Soon the people of Israel were very sad. They were afraid of their enemy and afraid to fight them. So they prayed to God. Would God hear them and rescue them?

God told the people, "I saved you from Egypt. I gave

you this land. But you won't obey Me. That's why I sent an enemy to fight you." The people of Israel didn't **deserve** God's help. They were sinful. But God had mercy on them even though they didn't **deserve** it. He said, "I will **deliver** them again."

God came to a man named Gideon. He said, "I have chosen you to fight Midian."

But Gideon said, "I can't fight! I'm afraid to fight! I'm not strong at all. I'm a very weak man!"

But God said, "I will be with you. You don't need to be strong or powerful because I am strong and powerful. You just need to trust Me. I will show Israel that I am the One who saves."

Gideon got some men together. Then he got **ready** to fight Midian. But God said, "You have too many men. Your army will think they can win the battle by **themselves**. They will think they don't need Me. Send most of your men home. I don't want many men because I will fight for you. I am the One who saves."

Most of Gideon's men went home. He **counted** the men who were left. There were only three hundred men left. And the army of Midian had over a hundred thousand men! Could three hundred men fight a hundred thousand soldiers? No, they couldn't. But God could!

Gideon gave each of his men a **torch** and a trumpet. Then he said, "Hide your **torch** in a jar and follow me." He went to the army of Midian. It was in the middle of the night. Everything was dark, so the people of Midian couldn't see them. Then Gideon told his men, "Break the jar so your **torches** shine out. Then blow your trumpet and shout. God will fight for us. He will defeat Midian!"

The men broke their jars and held up their **torches**. Then they blew their trumpets and shouted, "The **sword** of the Lord and Gideon!"

The people of Midian were terrified at this sound. They didn't know what was happening, so they started fighting each other. Then they all ran away. Gideon and his army chased them

and killed them. Then they praised God for saving them from their enemies. God had fought for them and saved them!

> *It happened on the same night that the* Lord
> *said to him, "Arise, go down against the camp,*
> *for I have delivered it into your hand."*
> *(Judges 7:9)*

Faith Lessons

God judged Israel — Israel didn't obey God, so He punished them. Sin is very wicked, and God must punish people for their sin. One day Jesus Christ will come and will judge all the world for sin. All people who sin must go to hell.

God is very merciful — The people of Israel kept sinning and sinning, but God had mercy on them. They didn't deserve His mercy, but He is a very merciful God. He saved them from their enemies. One day He would send Jesus. Jesus would die to save His people from sin. He is a very merciful God.

God is the One who saves — Israel couldn't fight against Midian. Only God could fight against them and win. We are like Israel. We can't fight against our sin. It is a very strong enemy. But God can fight against it. And He will win! We must trust God and must ask Him to save us from sin.

Vocabulary

deserve	themselves	sword
deliver	counted	
ready	torch	

CHAPTER 26

Hannah Prays for a Son

I n Israel there was a special place for people to come worship God. This place was called God's house. People from all over Israel came to this place to offer **sacrifices** to God. They did this to show that they were sorry for their sins. They did it to ask God to forgive them and to thank Him for protecting and loving them.

A man called Eli lived at the house of God with his family. Eli was a **priest**. A **priest** was a person who served God and who offered **sacrifices** to God. He did this for his own sins and for the sins of the people. The **priest** would teach the people what God said. He would serve God all his life and would make offerings for the people's sins. He was **supposed** to be a very good man. He was **supposed** to be a man who loved God and who obeyed His Law.

One day a woman came to the house of God. Her name was Hannah. She was very sad because she had no children. Her husband tried to make her happy, but she was still sad, so she came to God's house to pray. She prayed, "God, please give me a son! If You give me a son, I will give him back to You. I will bring him here to Your house, and he will live here and serve You all his life."

God heard Hannah's prayer. He had mercy on her, and He gave her a son. She named him Samuel. Samuel means "God heard."

Hannah was filled with great joy when Samuel was born. She praised God for being merciful and for hearing her prayer. She thanked Him and said, "My heart rejoices in God! No one is holy like He is. No one is strong like our God. He is able to kill and to make alive. He rules over all things He created. He makes some people poor and some people rich. He **does** all things. I was poor because I had no child, but now He has made me rich by giving me a son. I will praise Him because He is good!"

Hannah didn't forget her promise to God. When Samuel

was old enough, she brought him to the house of God and gave him to Eli the priest. She told him, "I asked God to give me a son. He heard my prayer and gave me Samuel. Now I will give him to God."

Eli took Samuel and taught the boy how to help in God's house. Samuel stayed there and lived with Eli.

Hannah went home, but God didn't forget her. He sent her many more children. Soon she had five more children. She was very thankful for God's goodness. He had not forgotten her prayer.

And Hannah prayed and said:
"My heart rejoices in the LORD; . . .
No one is holy like the LORD,
For there is none besides You,
Nor is there any rock like our God."
(1 Samuel 2:1-2)

Faith Lessons

Hannah prayed to God — Hannah wanted a son, but she couldn't create a son. Only God can do this, so Hannah prayed. She knew God is strong and powerful and is able to do all things. We must remember that we serve a strong and powerful God.

Hannah praised God — God gave Hannah a son, and she praised Him for it. She remembered to thank Him. She was filled with joy and love for God. We must praise Him just like Hannah did. We must remember to thank Him and worship Him, for He is a very good God.

God cares about little things — God made all the world, and it is a very big world. But God still sees every person in the world, and He cares for every single one of them. Hannah was just one little woman in Israel. But God cared about her. He heard her prayer and gave her a son. He is a very good God. He takes care of all His world, even the smallest things in it.

Vocabulary

sacrifice	does	smallest
priest	thankful	
suppose	forgotten	

CHAPTER 27

God Calls Samuel

Samuel worked in the house of God and helped Eli the priest. Eli had two sons, but his sons were wicked men. They **pretended** to be good men who served God, but they were very sinful. They did many sinful things, and Eli heard about it. He told his sons, "Why are you doing these things? All the people are talking about how wicked you are. You are sinning against God. You must **repent** and turn away from your sins. You must stop doing these things."

But Eli's sons wouldn't listen to their father. They rejected his **advice** and kept sinning.

Then a man came to Eli. He was sent by God, and he told Eli, "God sees the wicked sins your sons are doing. Why do you **despise** God and His ways? God will **despise** you. He will reject your family, and you will no longer be priests. God will raise up a faithful priest for Himself. This priest will follow God's ways and will love and obey Him."

One night Samuel went to bed. It was dark in the house of God, and everyone was asleep. Then Samuel heard a voice calling him. He ran to Eli. "Here I am," he said. "Why did

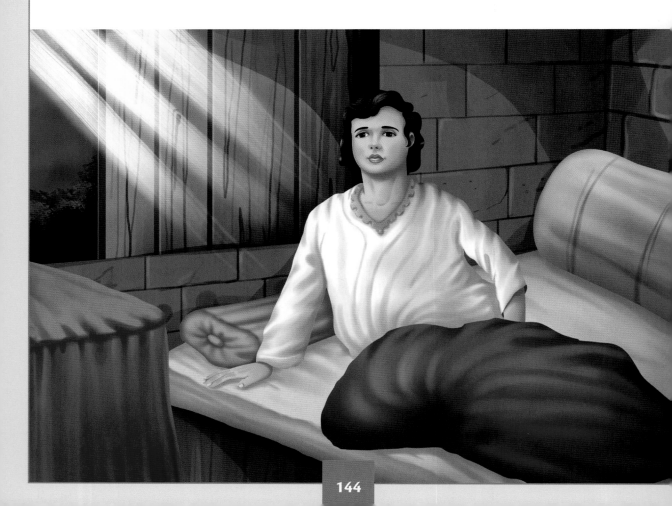

you call me?"

But Eli said, "I didn't call you. Go back to sleep."

Samuel went back to bed. But again he heard someone calling him. He got up and ran to Eli a **second** time. "Here I am!" he said.

"Go back to sleep," Eli told him. "I didn't call you."

Samuel went back to bed, but then he heard someone calling him again. He went to Eli. "Didn't you call me?" he asked. But Eli hadn't called him.

Suddenly, Eli **realized** who had called the boy. He said, "Samuel, God is calling you. When He calls again, you must tell Him that you are listening and that you will hear what He has to say."

Samuel went back to bed, and God called him again. Samuel said, "Speak, Lord, for Your servant is listening."

Then God said, "I told Eli that I would judge his family forever for their sins. His sons are wicked and will not **repent**, so I will judge them for their sins. I will kill all of them. Their sins will never be washed away."

Samuel was frightened when God said this. God is a holy God, and He hates sin. He will judge people for their sin.

God kept His promise to Eli. He promised to kill him and

his family, and He did. Eli died, and his sons died, too. This was God's judgment for their sin.

After Eli died, Samuel served at God's house. He wanted to be a man of God, and he knew that he must fear and obey God. He must listen to God's Word and follow in His ways.

Now the LORD came and stood and called as at other times, "Samuel! Samuel!" And Samuel answered, "Speak, for Your servant hears."
(1 Samuel 3:10)

Faith Lessons

God will judge for sin — God is a holy God. He is perfect, and He hates sin. He must punish people for their sin. He will judge all the world for sin. We cannot escape the judgment of God. We can't wash away our sins. Only Jesus can do this. We must run to Him to be saved.

Eli's sons would not listen to their father — Eli's sons sinned. Eli told them to stop sinning, but they didn't listen to him. This was very wicked. Then God killed them all. We must not be like Eli's sons. We must listen when someone tells us to stop sinning. We must be quick to repent and turn away from our sins and turn back to God.

All priests sin — All people sin. Even priests sin because they are human. But one day God would send a priest who would never sin. This would be a perfect priest who would make a perfect sacrifice for His people. This priest was Jesus.

Vocabulary

pretend	despise	judgment
repent	second	
advice	realize	

CHAPTER 28

Israel Wants a King

When Samuel grew into a man, he ruled over Israel. He taught the people God's Law and showed them how to live. When he got old, the people came to him. They were afraid of what would happen when he died. They said, "Who will rule over us when you die? We don't want your sons to rule over us. We want a king instead. Give us a king! Then we will be just like all the other nations. A king will protect us and keep us safe. Find us a king and make him a ruler over us!"

Samuel wasn't happy with the people's request. The people weren't satisfied with the rulers God gave them, so they wanted something new. They wanted a king. But the Lord told Samuel, "The people haven't rejected you. They have rejected Me. They keep rejecting Me again and again. They don't want Me to **reign** over them, so they are asking for a king." Then God said, "Do what the people ask. But first, **warn** them about what will happen if they have a king."

Samuel told the people, "If you want a king, God will give you one. But the king will take things that are yours. He will tax you and make you pay him. You will have to work for him, too. He will make you work hard, and then you will be sorry you asked for a king. You will wish you didn't have a king, but it will be too late then."

The people didn't believe Samuel. They thought a new ruler would fix their nation, so they said, "We still want a king! He will fight our battles for us, and we can follow him. Then we'll be safe." They trusted in a king to save them, but they didn't trust in God.

Samuel told the people, "You have rejected God. He brought you out of Egypt. He saved you when you were slaves. Then He gave you this good land He promised you. He has saved you from all your enemies. He has always protected you, but now you say, 'Give us a king!' God will give you a king, but this king won't save you."

Then God chose a man from Israel. His name was Saul.

Saul was a tall, **handsome** man. The people liked him. He looked like a king. He looked like a strong man to save them. When the people saw him, they shouted happily. Here was a good king for them! But would Saul be a good king for Israel? What do you think?

> The people refused to obey the voice of Samuel; and they said, "No, but we will have a king over us, that we also may be like all the nations, and that our king may judge us and go out before us and fight our battles."
> (1 Samuel 8:19-20)

Faith Lessons

Israel trusted in a king — The people wanted a king who could rule over them and protect them. They were foolish to hope that a king could save them. Only God can save. We must not trust in our rulers to save us. We must trust in God. He is the One who saves.

Israel wanted to be like other nations — Israel wanted to be like all the other nations. This was sin. They were God's people, and God didn't want them to be like other people. God wants His people to walk in His ways and follow Him. His people should want a godly nation, not a nation like all the wicked nations in the world.

Israel wasn't satisfied with what God gave them — God gave Israel rulers, but the people weren't satisfied. They wanted a new ruler. They thought a new ruler would fix their nation and their problems. But only God can fix a nation's problems.

Vocabulary

instead	reign	happily
request	warn	
satisfied	handsome	

CHAPTER 29

God Chooses a King

The people of Israel thought Saul would be a good king. He was a strong, handsome man. He looked like a good king on the outside. But on the inside, he was a wicked man. He didn't obey God.

Samuel was very sorry Saul wasn't a good king. But God told him, "Don't be sorry about Saul. I have rejected him. But I have chosen another man to be king. He will be a good king and will love Me."

Samuel went to a city called Bethlehem. God told him he would find the new king here. The king would be a son of a man in the city named Jesse.

Samuel went to Jesse's house. He looked at Jesse's oldest son. "This is a big, strong man!" he said. "Surely God will

choose this man to be His new king!"

But God said, "Don't look at this man's **appearance** or his size. I don't look at those things. I don't look at the things you look at. You see what a man looks like on the outside, but I look at his heart."

Then Samuel looked at the next son. "Maybe God will choose this one!" he thought. But God said, "I don't want him, either."

Samuel looked at seven of **Jesse's** sons, but God didn't choose any of them.

"Don't you have any more sons?" Samuel asked.

"I have one more," **Jesse** said. "He's the **youngest**, and he's in the field watching the sheep."

"Call him," Samuel said.

Jesse called his **youngest** son from the field. His name was David. When he came in, God told Samuel, "This is the one I have chosen! This will be the new king for Israel."

Samuel told David that God would make him king. But David wasn't the king yet. Saul was still king, and he still ruled over all Israel.

Soon an enemy came to attack Israel. The enemy had a giant named Goliath. All the men of Israel were afraid to fight Goliath, but David wasn't afraid. He said, "God is strong and powerful. He can kill a giant. I'm not afraid of Goliath."

God blessed David and protected him. David killed Goliath and cut off his head. Then Israel wasn't afraid anymore. The people fought their enemies and won a mighty victory.

King Saul watched David kill Goliath. Then he asked one of his army **commanders**, "Who is this young man David?"

The **commander** said, "I don't know, O king."

"Find out who he is," Saul said. He wanted to know more about David.

Soon all the people in Israel were talking about David. He killed Goliath, and he helped win a mighty victory. Now all the people loved him.

King Saul found out who David was. Then he told David to stay at the **palace** with him. He made him a **commander** over part of his army.

> But the LORD said to Samuel, "Do not look at his appearance or at his physical stature, because I have refused him. For the LORD does not see as man sees; for man looks at the outward appearance, but the LORD looks at the heart."
>
> *(1 Samuel 16:7)*

Faith Lessons

God looks on the inside — Samuel looked at Jesse's oldest son and saw that he was big and strong. He thought this would be a good king, but God said no. God didn't look at the outside of the person. He looked at the heart. God looks for a person who loves and obeys Him, not a person who is big and strong.

God sees everything — Samuel couldn't see inside Jesse's sons. He didn't know what was in their hearts. But God knows. He sees things we can't see. We can't see inside a person, but God sees inside every person in the whole world! Nothing can hide from Him.

God rules all things — The people of Israel were afraid of their enemy Goliath. But David wasn't afraid. He knew that God rules all things. God was able to destroy the giant even though he was such a big man. We must remember that God rules everything. That means we don't ever need to be afraid.

Vocabulary

Bethlehem	appearance	palace
Jesse	youngest	
surely	commander	

CHAPTER 30

A Jealous King

David served in the army of King Saul. God blessed him. He let David win many battles. An enemy was fighting against Israel. The enemy was called the Philistines. David fought the Philistines and won.

The people of Israel were very glad that David won the battle. They started dancing and singing. They played music and shouted for joy. They said, "Saul has killed thousands of enemies. But now David has killed tens of thousands!"

King Saul heard the people singing, and he wasn't happy. He didn't like them saying David was better than he was. This made him very jealous. "They say David killed tens of thousands. But they say I only killed thousands!" he said angrily. Saul became so angry that he decided to kill David.

Saul had a long spear in his hand, so he threw it and tried to kill David with it. But David jumped out of the way and escaped. Saul was still angry. He sent some of his men to David's house to kill him.

David found out that the men were coming. He had to escape, or he would be killed. If he tried to go out his front

door, Saul's men would see him and **capture** him. So David waited until it was night. Then his wife helped him climb out a window and sneak away into the darkness. No one saw him go, so he escaped out of the city.

When Saul's men went into the house to **arrest** David, he wasn't there. He had **already** escaped!

Saul was **furious** that David had gotten away. He gathered his soldiers together and chased after David to kill him.

David was scared when he heard that Saul was coming with his soldiers. He was afraid Saul would find him and kill him, so he ran far, far away. He went into the wilderness to hide from Saul. There were many mountains and caves in the wilderness. David hoped he would be safe here. Maybe King Saul wouldn't find him.

What do you think? Will Saul find David? Will he kill him? Will David become king? Did God forget His promise? What will happen next?

Then Saul was very angry, and the saying displeased him;
and he said, "They have ascribed to David ten thousands,
and to me they have ascribed only thousands."
(1 Samuel 18:8)

Faith Lessons

Saul was jealous of David — God blessed David. He beat his enemies. This made Saul jealous. But he shouldn't have been jealous. He should have been glad that God blessed David. We should never be jealous when God blesses other people. We should rejoice. Then we should thank God for His blessings.

David trusted God — God promised to make David king, but David wasn't king yet. Instead, Saul was trying to kill him. Now David had to run away. But he still trusted God. He knew God would keep His promise one day. He would still make David king.

God kept David safe — Saul wanted to kill David. He threw a spear at him. Then he sent soldiers to kill him. But God stopped Saul. He didn't let Saul's plans work. God always protected David. He is a powerful God. He can always protect His people from their enemies.

Vocabulary

Philistine	capture	furious
music	arrest	
jealous	already	

CHAPTER 31

David Lets God Be the Judge

For a long time, David lived in the wilderness. Other men came and lived with him. Soon David had a small army of men with him. The men knew David was a good man. They knew Saul was wrong to try to kill him, so they followed David.

But King Saul was still angry at David. He was afraid David would become king, so he tried to kill him again and again.

One day a man came to King Saul. "I know where David is hiding!" the man said. King Saul gathered his army together and went out to find David. He journeyed to the wilderness and camped with his army.

David found out that Saul had come with his army to kill him. David waited until it was night, and then he took Abishai, one of his men, and crept up to Saul's camp. Everyone in the camp was sleeping soundly. No one heard David come, and no one knew he was there. David looked around and saw everyone fast asleep. Even Saul was asleep, lying on the ground with his spear beside his head.

Abishai saw King Saul, too. He whispered to David, "God has delivered your enemy into your hand! Now we can kill Saul and escape without anyone knowing we were here!"

Then Abishai said, "Please let me take Saul's spear, and I will kill him with it! Then your enemy will be dead, and you will never have to fear him again."

But David said, "No, don't kill him. God chose Saul to be king. Even if he's a wicked man, he is still the king. Do you think you would be free from guilt if you killed him? No, it would be sin! We must not hurt him."

David looked down at where Saul was sleeping. He could easily kill him, but he knew it wouldn't be the right thing to do. "Saul is trying to kill me," he said, "but I will not hurt him. If God wants to stop him, God can kill him easily. But I will not do it."

Then David took Saul's spear and water jug and crept back out of the camp.

After he was outside, David climbed a hill far from Saul's camp. Then he called to the leader of Saul's army. "Wake up!" he called. "Why are you sleeping? Why don't you protect your king? Someone crept into your camp and might have killed your king, but you were asleep the whole time!"

Then David said, "Where is the king's spear and water jug? Can you find them?"

Now the army was awake. Saul was awake, too. He heard David's voice and knew who it was. "Is that you, David?" he asked.

"It is, O king," David replied. "Why are you hunting me to kill me? What evil have I done? Please listen to me. I have done no wrong, and yet you're trying to kill me. I could have killed you tonight, but I didn't because I'm not your enemy. Please stop trying to kill me."

Saul heard David's words and knew they were true.

"I have sinned," he said. "Return, my son David. I will harm you no more. Now I see that my life is **precious** to you because you didn't kill me. I have acted like a fool."

David gave Saul's spear and water jug back. Then Saul took his army and went home. He stopped hunting for David, but David stayed in the wilderness. Saul said he was sorry, but could David trust him? David wasn't sure yet **whether** Saul would keep his promise or not.

> *Then Saul said, "I have sinned. Return, my son David. For I will harm you no more, because my life was precious in your eyes this day. Indeed I have played the fool and erred exceedingly."*
> *(1 Samuel 26:21)*

Faith Lessons

David waited for God — Abishai wanted to kill Saul right away. But David told him, "No, you must not kill him. That would be sin. We must wait for God to judge him." David knew Saul was wrong, but David couldn't punish Saul. He had to wait for God to do that.

Saul acted like a fool — A fool is a person who will not listen to God's Word. He will not obey God's Law. He lives how he likes to live, and he **doesn't** care about God. We must not be like Saul. We must not act like fools. Let us always listen to God's Word. Let us follow Jesus Christ, who is the Wisdom of God.

Saul was not a good king — God let Saul be king, but Saul was not a good king. One day God would send a very good king to rule His people. He would send a perfect King, and this King is Jesus.

Vocabulary

soundly	easily	whether
whispered	replied	doesn't
guilt	precious	

CHAPTER 32

David Becomes King and Worships God

King Saul promised he wouldn't try to kill David anymore, but he lied. He took his army and came back later to hunt David and kill him. Samuel told Saul that God was not pleased with him. He told the king to repent and turn from his sins, but Saul refused to listen. He turned away from God and did **whatever** he wanted to do. God judged Saul for his sins. He sent an enemy against Israel. Saul went to fight the enemy and was killed in the battle. His sons were killed, too.

After Saul died, the Israelites chose David as their new king. God had promised to give David the **kingdom** of Israel, and now He kept His promise. David rejoiced and thanked God for His goodness. He praised God for keeping him safe from Saul and for making him king.

David knew that it is very good to praise God. It is good to thank Him for what He has done for us. It's good to remember what God did. David wrote many songs about God and about what He did for His people. These songs are called **psalms**.

David sang:

"I will praise You, my God and King.
I will bless Your name forever.
Every day I will bless You.
The Lord is great, and greatly to be praised."

David wrote his **psalms** down and **recorded** them in a book. He did this so that his children and grandchildren could read them and praise God. He did this so that people living a long, long time after him could still use these **psalms** to worship God. David wrote:

> *"One generation will praise God's works*
> *And will tell the next generation about Him.*
> *I will talk about God's great goodness,*
> *And I will tell others about His greatness.*
>
> *"The Lord is gracious and full of compassion.*
> *He is slow to anger and great in mercy.*
> *He is good to all,*
> *And His tender mercies are over all His world.*
>
> *"All Your works will praise You, O Lord,*
> *And your saints will bless You.*
> *They will speak of the glory of Your kingdom*
> *And will talk about Your power.*
> *Your kingdom is an everlasting kingdom,*
> *And Your rule lasts forever and ever."*

David remembered that God saved him from Saul. God kept David safe even when wicked men tried to kill him. David sang to the Lord:

"The Lord protects those who fall.

He is righteous in all His ways.

He is near to all who call on Him in truth.

He will answer those who fear Him.

He will hear their cry and save them.

"The Lord preserves all those who love Him,

But He will destroy the wicked.

My mouth will speak the praises of the Lord,

And all flesh will bless His holy name

Forever and ever!"

> *My mouth shall speak the praise of the Lord,*
> *And all flesh shall bless His holy name*
> *Forever and ever.*
> *(Psalm 145:21)*

Faith Lessons

God judged Saul for his sins — Saul sinned and refused to turn back to God, so God killed him. We must not be like Saul. We must turn away from our sins and turn to God. We must ask Him to save us from our sins.

David thanked God for keeping His promise — God saved David from his enemies, and David thanked God for this. He didn't forget to praise God. We must not forget, either. We should always praise God for what He has done for us. He is a great and very good God!

It's good for us to read and sing the psalms — David and other men wrote many psalms. God recorded these psalms in the Bible so that we can still have them today. It is very good to read these psalms. It's good to sing them, too. They teach us about the mighty God we serve.

Vocabulary

whatever	greatly	generation
kingdom	greatness	righteous
psalm	record	

CHAPTER 33

God Makes a Covenant with David

When David became king, God made his kingdom strong. David fought many battles. He fought against his enemies and won. He became a great king in Israel, and Israel became a great nation. David ruled over the nation, and the land had **peace**.

Then God spoke to David. He said, "When you were a young man, I took you from the fields. I called you when you were keeping watch over your sheep. You were a **shepherd** of sheep, but I made you a ruler over My people, over all Israel. I have been with you **wherever** you went. I saved you from all your enemies. I have blessed you, and you are a great man now."

Then God said, "I will make a covenant with you. When you die, I will make your son king after you. He will reign over Israel, and I will establish his kingdom. I will set up a kingdom that will last forever. Your son will rule, and I will be a Father to him. If he sins, I will punish him for his sins. But I will not take My mercy away from him like I did with Saul. I will establish your children on the throne forever."

David was astonished to hear what God said. He was very surprised. David knew he was a sinful man. He didn't deserve God's mercy. He didn't deserve God's blessing or His covenant. But God is a very merciful and gracious God. He loved David, and He had mercy on him.

David prayed: "Who am I, O God? I am nothing! And yet You called me and made me a ruler over this nation. Now You have promised to bless my children after me. What can I say? You are great, O Lord! There is no one like You. Nor is there any God besides You!"

David said, "O Lord God, You are God, and Your words are true. You have promised this goodness to me Your servant. I will trust in Your word, for You have spoken it. I know that You will bless my house forever."

David was a sinful man, but he trusted God. He knew that

his sons would be sinful, too. But God would still keep His promise. One day God would raise up a Man to be king over His people forever. This Man would never sin. Do you know who this Man is? He would come from David's family, and He will rule over God's people forever.

> *"When your days are fulfilled and you rest with your fathers,*
> *I will set up your seed after you, who will come from your*
> *body, and I will establish his kingdom. He shall build a house*
> *for My name, and I will establish the throne of*
> *his kingdom forever."*
> *(2 Samuel 7:12-13)*

Faith Lessons

David praised God for His power — David was king over all Israel. But he knew that he hadn't made himself king. God had made him king. Now David was king over a mighty nation, but David's power didn't do this. God did this. It was only through the power of God. We must also remember that our own power can't save us or make us great. Only God can do this. He is a mighty God, and He rules over all.

God made a promise — God promised to establish a kingdom forever. This kingdom is the kingdom of Jesus Christ. God is full of mercy and grace. He set up a kingdom to rule forever. He calls people from all over the world to be a part of His people. These people all sin, but God still has mercy on them and makes them His own. He made a promise to David, and He will keep that promise forever! Let us praise Him for this!

Vocabulary

peace
shepherd
wherever

covenant
establish
astonish

gracious

CHAPTER 34

Elisha and an Oily Miracle

After David grew old and died, his son became king. He was a good king, and he ruled over Israel. But after he died, his sons began to rule. Some men were good, but others were wicked. Many wicked kings reigned in Israel. These kings didn't fear God or obey Him. They refused to follow His Law and listen to His Word.

God punished Israel for these sins. He sent enemy nations to attack them. Then He sent a famine on the land. There was no food to eat. Just like Egypt, God judged Israel when they sinned.

But God didn't forget His promise. He sent men to teach the people God's Word. These men were called prophets.

They explained to the people what sin was. Then they told the people to repent and turn back to God.

One **prophet** was named **Elisha**. He feared God and trusted Him. Many men came to **Elisha** to learn about God. **Elisha** taught them God's Word. He taught them to love and obey God.

One of the men that **Elisha** taught was married. He had a wife and two sons. But then the man died. He had **borrowed** money when he was alive, and he hadn't paid the money back. Now that he was dead, the man he **borrowed** money from came to his wife. She was a widow because her husband was dead. "Pay me back the money!" the man said.

The widow didn't have any money, so the man **threatened** to take her two sons away. He would make the sons work for him until they paid back the money they **owed** him.

The widow didn't want to lose her two sons, so she went to **Elisha**. "Please help me!" she said. "You know my husband feared God and loved Him. But now he is dead, and this man wants to take away my sons!"

Elisha asked the widow, "What do you have in your house?"

"I only have a jar of oil," she said. "That's the only thing I own."

Elisha told her, "Go borrow empty pots and jars from all your friends and neighbors. Don't get just a few. Get as many vessels as you can. Then go inside your house with your sons and pour your oil into the empty pots and jars."

The widow didn't understand. How could her little jar of oil fill up all those empty pots and jars? But she did what Elisha told her to. She borrowed as many as she could. Then she poured out her oil into all the empty pots and jars. There wasn't much oil in her jar, but God made a miracle. He filled all the vessels with her little bit of oil!

The widow filled up all the empty pots and jars. Then she ran and told Elisha, "They're all full of oil!"

Elisha said, "Go sell the oil. Then you will have enough money to pay off what your husband borrowed. You'll also have enough money left over for you and your sons to live on."

A certain woman of the wives of the sons of the prophets cried out to Elisha, saying, "Your servant my husband is dead, and you know that your servant feared the LORD. And the creditor is coming to take my two sons to be his slaves."

(2 Kings 4:1)

Faith Lessons

God remembered His promise — The kings of Israel sinned. The people of Israel sinned, too. God punished them for their sins, but He didn't forget His promise. He sent prophets to preach to the people. He sent them to teach God's ways to the people. God is very merciful. When we sin, He sends people to tell us to stop sinning and turn back to Him.

God had a plan for the widow — The widow was very sad when her husband died. She was sad when the man came to take away her sons, too. But God had a plan. He blessed the widow and showed how powerful He was when He filled the jars with oil. The widow saw God's mighty works in her time of sadness. God will often teach us many things in times when we are sad or in times of trouble.

God has compassion on His people — The woman's husband feared and obeyed God. God saw this, and He didn't forget the man's family after he died. God protected the widow and her sons. He is a Father to the fatherless, and He is a protector of widows. He is a very good and loving God. Let us praise Him!

Vocabulary

prophet	threaten	miracle
Elisha	owe	trouble
borrow	vessel	

CHAPTER 35

God Heals an Enemy

When the people of Israel sinned, God sent enemies to attack them. One enemy nation fought battles against them and won. They took some people from Israel **captive** and made them slaves. This nation was called **Syria**.

The commander of **Syria's** army was a man named **Naaman** (nay-man). **Naaman** was a strong and brave man. He fought against Israel and took many **captives**. One of the people he captured was a little girl. **Naaman** brought the girl to his home. He gave her to his wife as a slave. The little girl served **Naaman's** wife.

Naaman was a strong man, but he had a problem. He had

a bad **disease** called **leprosy**. He was a **leper**, and no doctor could make him well. No one could help him.

The girl from Israel saw that her master was sick. She told **Naaman's** wife, "There is a prophet in Israel who could heal your husband." She knew that Elisha could ask God to heal her master. God was powerful enough to heal him even though the doctors couldn't.

When Naaman heard about Elisha, he called his servants and prepared his horse and chariot. Then he put many gold and silver coins in bags. He took fine clothes as gifts, too. Then he went to Elisha's house in Israel.

Elisha knew that Naaman had come. He knew he wanted to be healed. So he sent a servant outside and said, "Tell Naaman to go wash in the Jordan River seven times. Then he will be healed from his leprosy."

The servant told Naaman what Elisha said. As Naaman listened, his face got red with anger. "Why does he want me to go wash in a filthy river?" he asked angrily. "I thought he would come out and call on his God and heal me right here!"

Naaman was so furious that he turned his chariot around and left. He decided to go right back to Syria. But his servants said to him, "If the prophet had told you to do something very hard, wouldn't you do it? So why don't you go wash in the river like he told you? Please try it."

Naaman agreed to try, so he went to the Jordan. Then he washed seven times like Elisha had said. When he was done, he looked at his body. It was healed!

Now Naaman was full of joy. He knew that Elisha's God was the true God, for He had healed him. All other gods were **useless**. But the God of Israel was true!

Naaman raced back to Elisha's house. He said, "Now I know your God is the true God. There is no God in all the earth except in Israel!"

He said, "I will never make an offering to any other god. I won't make any sacrifices to anyone else, either. The God of Israel is the Lord, for He is the true God."

> *And he returned to the man of God, he and all his aides,*
> *and came and stood before him; and he said, "Indeed, now I*
> *know that there is no God in all the earth, except in Israel."*
> (2 Kings 5:15)

Faith Lessons

A little girl trusted God — The little slave girl trusted God and obeyed Him. She didn't want to be a slave, but she still served her master. She even tried to help him when he was sick. She had compassion on her enemies just like God does.

God healed Naaman — Naaman was an enemy of Israel. But God still healed him. He is a God full of grace.

God is a mighty God — Naaman knew the God of Israel was the only true God because He could heal. No doctor could help Naaman or fix his disease, but God could. No one on earth could heal him, but God could easily do it, and He did. He is a mighty, powerful God. Let us praise Him!

Naaman worshiped God — Naaman was from Syria. He wasn't part of Israel, but he still worshiped God. God calls people from every nation to Himself. He chooses men and women and boys and girls from all over the world to be His people. Let us thank Him for this!

Vocabulary

captive	disease	chariot
Syria	leprosy	useless
Naaman	leper	

CHAPTER 36

Elisha's Servant Tries to Hide from God

Naaman was filled with joy when he was healed. He took out bags of silver and gold and the fine clothes he brought. Then he gave them to Elisha. "Please take a gift from your servant," he said.

But Elisha shook his head. "I won't take your money or your gifts," he said. He knew that God had healed Naaman. He didn't want Naaman to pay him for the healing. God healed him out of His mercy. He didn't want to be paid.

"I will always worship your God," Naaman said. "He is the only true God." Then he got back into his chariot to go home to Syria.

Elisha's servant watched Naaman leave. When Elisha

went back inside his house, the servant waited outside. He said, "Naaman has lots of gold and silver. He has lots of nice things. I'd like to have some of those things." So he ran after Naaman's chariot. He didn't tell Elisha where he was going.

Naaman saw the man running after him, so he stopped. "Is everything **alright**?" he asked.

"Yes," the servant said. "But some **guests** just came to

the house, and Elisha needs something to give them," he lied. "He sent me after you. Can you give our **guests** a little money and some new clothes?"

"Yes! Please take as much as you **desire**," Naaman said. He pulled out the silver and gold and gave it to the servant. Then he gave him the fine clothes, too. He gave him so much that he couldn't carry it all. The money and clothes were so **heavy** that Naaman sent two men with the servant to carry them for him.

When he got near his house, the servant took the silver and gold and clothes and hid them. Then he sent the men back to Naaman.

Elisha was inside when the servant came back. "Where did you go?" he asked.

"I didn't go anywhere," the servant lied. He had hidden the silver and gold so Elisha didn't see it, but God saw it.

"God knows what you did," Elisha said. "He saw you run after Naaman and stop his chariot. He saw the silver and gold and clothes you took from him. He heard your lies. Now He will judge you for your sins. From now on, you will be a leper like Naaman was. You and your children will be lepers forever."

As soon as Elisha finished speaking, the servant looked down at his body. It was covered with the terrible disease. He was a leper!

But Gehazi, the servant of Elisha the man of God, said, "Look, my master has spared Naaman this Syrian, while not receiving from his hands what he brought; but as the LORD lives, I will run after him and take something from him."
(2 Kings 5:20)

Faith Lessons

God gives His gifts freely — Naaman wanted to pay Elisha for healing him, but Elisha said no. God doesn't want to be paid for His kindness. We could never pay Him enough for what He does for us. We must thank Him and praise Him. We must worship Him like Naaman did.

Elisha's servant was a wicked man — Elisha's servant thought he could get away with his sin. He pretended to be good. He thought nobody would find out about what he did. But he was wrong. We must not be like him. We must not think we can hide our sin.

God chooses His own people — Elisha's servant was a man of Israel. He was part of the people of God, but he was a wicked man. God rejected him and judged him for his sin. But He chose Naaman, who was a Syrian. God chooses whoever He wants to be His people.

Vocabulary

alright	heavy	whoever
guest	freely	
desire	nobody	

CHAPTER 37

Israel Refuses to Repent

God sent prophets to the kings of Israel. He sent prophets to the people, too. The prophets preached **repentance**. They begged the nation to turn from its sins. They called people to turn back to God. But the kings and the people didn't listen. They kept sinning. They did many wicked things. They worshiped false gods. They killed **innocent** people. They broke God's Law and lived very wicked lives.

God waited many, many years for His people to repent. He waited for them to turn back to Him. God was very **patient** with Israel. But the nation refused to repent. They would not listen. They refused to turn back to God.

Then God said, "I made a promise. I promised to bless you if you obeyed Me. I promised to make you a great nation. I promised to save you from all your enemies. But you will not obey. You have turned away from Me. You worship false gods. You walk in very wicked ways."

Then God said, "Now listen to what I will tell you. I will punish you for your sins. I will send such judgment on you that people will be afraid when they hear about it. Other nations will be shocked when they hear how I have destroyed you. When you clean a plate, you take a cloth and wipe the plate clean. That's what I will do with you. I will wipe you off the face of the earth. I will send strong enemies to kill you. You have turned away from Me. And now I will turn away from you."

God was very **patient** with Israel. But now He sent His judgment on them. Enemies attacked and killed them. They **ruined** the land and made the people slaves. God judged Israel and destroyed their nation.

But did God forget His promise? He made a promise to Abraham. He promised to make a mighty nation out of his children. God didn't forget His promise. He saved some people in Israel. Even when He sent judgment on the nation,

He had mercy on some of them. He saved these people and kept them safe.

One of these men was Daniel. Daniel was a young man when God sent enemies to Israel. The enemies killed many people and made slaves of the rest. Daniel was caught and became a **prisoner**. Then he was taken to a far country called **Babylon** (bab-i-lon). He would live in this country for the rest of his life. He would never see his parents again. He would never see his home again. But God kept him safe even in a **foreign** land. He promised to save a people for Himself, and He saved Daniel as one of His people.

"I will wipe Jerusalem as one wipes a dish, wiping it and turning it upside down."

(2 Kings 21:13)

Faith Lessons

God will judge the world — The people of Israel thought they could get away with their sin. They thought God wouldn't punish them. But they were wrong. God sent judgment on them and destroyed them. God will always punish people for their sin. One day He will judge the whole world for sin.

God is very patient — God was patient with Israel. He waited a long, long time for them to turn from their sins.

God remembers His promises — God promised to make a special people. These would be His very own people. He would keep this promise even though He destroyed Israel. He will choose a people to be His own. These people will come from every nation. Let us thank God for this! Let us praise Him because He keeps His promises!

Vocabulary

repentance	ruin	foreign
innocent	prisoner	
patient	Babylon	

CHAPTER 38

Daniel Explains a Dream

Daniel was captured by the enemies of Israel. These men took him to Babylon. Then they put him in a special school. They wanted Daniel to become a wise man who could serve the king of Babylon. The king's name was Nebuchadnezzar (Neb-u-cud-nezz-er).

Daniel lived in Babylon and served the king. But he didn't forget God. He knew he had to obey the king, but he had to obey God first.

One night the king had a dream. He didn't know what the dream meant, so he called all his wise men. He asked them to tell him the dream. Then he wanted them to interpret it. He wanted them to tell him what the dream meant.

The wise men couldn't tell the king what his dream was. The king got angry and said, "If you can't tell me what I dreamed, I will kill you all!" He ordered his soldiers to kill all the wise men in Babylon.

The soldiers came to kill Daniel. But Daniel knew that God could tell what the king's dream was. He asked the king to give him a little time. Then he prayed to God and asked Him to tell him what the dream was and what it meant. God answered his prayer. Daniel praised God. Then he went to the king.

Daniel said, "O king, no one can tell you what you dreamed. This is a secret that only God knows. But God can tell you what you dreamed. You dreamed that you saw a large statue. This statue was beautiful. It was made of gold and silver and iron and clay. Then you saw a large stone. The stone hit the statue and destroyed it. Then the stone became a huge mountain and filled the whole earth."

Daniel said, "This is what your dream means. You are a great king, and you have a large kingdom. You are the gold on the statue. After you die, other kings will come. Your kingdom will be ruined. But new kingdoms will rise up after yours. These are the silver and iron and clay on the statue.

These kingdoms will all be destroyed, too. But one day the God of heaven will set up a kingdom that will never be destroyed. This is the stone. This kingdom will destroy all other kingdoms. It will break them in pieces. But it will last forever."

King **Nebuchadnezzar** was shocked to hear what Daniel said. He said, "Truly your God is the God of all gods! He is the Lord of all kings! He reveals **secrets** that no one knows. He must be God because He told you what I dreamed."

Then the king made Daniel a ruler in Babylon. He knew that Daniel's God was the only true God.

The king answered Daniel, and said, "Truly your God is the God of gods, the Lord of kings, and a revealer of secrets, since you could reveal this secret."

(Daniel 2:47)

Faith Lessons

God is Lord over all the earth — The king of Babylon worshiped false gods. But God showed him who the true God was. He sent a dream, and then He sent Daniel to interpret the dream. Then the king knew that God is the only true God. He is Lord over all nations and all the earth.

God will build His kingdom — The king of Babylon had a very big kingdom. He was a powerful king, and he ruled over many people. But God would destroy his kingdom. God destroys all wicked kingdoms of men. But He is building His own kingdom. This kingdom will last forever. It will never be destroyed.

God is a merciful God — God judged Israel because they sinned. But He had mercy on some of Israel. He had mercy on Daniel and protected him. Daniel trusted and worshiped God. We should trust and worship Him, too. We should thank Him for His mercy.

Vocabulary

school	secret	iron
Nebuchadnezzar	statue	
interpret	beautiful	

CHAPTER 39

God's Story about His Sheep

The people of Israel didn't live in their own land anymore. God had punished them for their sins, and now they were scattered in many foreign lands. They lived in the lands of their enemies, and they couldn't go home. They were very sad and wished they could go home, but they couldn't. They were stuck in the land of their enemies.

God sent prophets to the people. His prophets told the people to repent and turn from their sins. The prophets said, "God is a merciful God. Stop sinning, and turn back to God. Ask Him to save you."

But the leaders of the people didn't want to turn back to

God. They didn't want to lead the people in God's ways. All they thought about was themselves.

God saw this, so He told His people a story. This is the story:

God had a flock of sheep. He **hired** shepherds to watch the sheep. But the shepherds didn't watch the sheep. **Instead**, they killed the sheep and ate them. Then they took the **wool**

from the sheep and made clothes for themselves.

Some of the sheep were hurt, but the shepherds didn't care. They didn't **bandage** their **wounds** or take care of the sheep when they were sick. Some of the sheep **wandered** away and got lost, but the shepherds didn't do anything about it. They didn't bring the lost sheep back to the flock. When a sheep got stuck in some thorns, the shepherds just left it there to die. They were selfish and cruel. Soon the flock of sheep was scattered all over the earth, and no one helped them or went to rescue them. **Wolves** attacked the sheep and ate them, but the shepherds didn't care.

God saw what the shepherds were doing. He said, "My shepherds are not caring for the sheep. They are feeding themselves and are only caring about themselves. Because of this, I will rescue My sheep from these wicked shepherds. I will search for My sheep and will find the ones that are lost. I will rescue them from all the countries where they **wandered** to, and I will bring them back to their own land. I will feed them there, and I will give them good **pasture**. I will heal the **wounded** sheep, and I will strengthen the sick ones. But I will destroy the wicked shepherds and will judge them."

Then God said, "I will save My flock. And I will set a new

shepherd over them. He shall feed them. He will be a good shepherd. He will protect My sheep from the wild animals and will save them from all danger. Then they will never be afraid again. They will know that I am the Lord their God, and they are My people."

This was the story God told His people. Do you know who the sheep were? Do you know who the wicked shepherds were?

God promised to send a good shepherd. This new shepherd would love the sheep and would protect them. He would even give His life to save the sheep. Do you know who this shepherd is?

"I will save My flock, and they shall no longer be a prey; and I will judge between sheep and sheep. I will establish one shepherd over them, and he shall feed them."
(Ezekiel 34:22-23)

Faith Lessons

God will judge wicked people — The leaders of Israel didn't lead the people in God's ways. They didn't fear God or obey Him. They were wicked, and God judged them for this.

God's people are like sheep — God told a story about sheep. The sheep were His people. His people wandered away from God just like sheep wander away and get lost. His people did foolish things just like sheep do silly things and get stuck in thorns or fall off cliffs. But God cares for His people. He knows they are foolish like sheep, so He helps them.

Jesus is the Good Shepherd — God loves His sheep, and He sent a perfect shepherd to protect them and save them. This shepherd is Jesus. Let us thank God for sending Jesus to be our shepherd!

Vocabulary

hire	bandage	wolf
instead	wound	pasture
wool	wandered	

CHAPTER 40

Nehemiah Cries Out to God

God's people were scattered in many lands far from Israel. One man from Israel was named Nehemiah (Ne-he-mi-ah). He lived in the land of his enemies and served the king there. He had a special job because he was the king's cupbearer. A cupbearer was a person who served the king at his meals and gave him his cup to drink from.

One day a man came from Israel. Nehemiah asked what the land was like since God judged it. "It's very bad," the man replied. "The walls of our greatest city are broken down. The gates are all burned up. Nothing but rubble is left. There are a few people left, but they have no one to protect them."

Nehemiah was very sad to hear what the man said. He

started to cry when he thought about his people being in trouble. He was filled with **sorrow** when he thought about all their cities being destroyed and burned down.

Nehemiah cried and cried. But he also prayed. He said, "Lord God, please hear me. We have sinned. We are Your people, but we sinned against You. Now You have judged us for our sin. You were right to judge us. We were very wicked.

But please have mercy on us. We want to fear Your name. We want to follow You. Please have mercy and let us go back to our land. Let us **rebuild** our towns that are destroyed."

After his prayer, **Nehemiah** went to serve the king. He took a cup of wine and gave it to the king. But the king saw he was very sad. "What's wrong?" he asked.

Nehemiah was afraid. The king might get angry at him for being sad. He prayed **silently** to God, "Please don't let the king get angry!" Then he said, "O king, I am sad because the land of my fathers is destroyed. The cities are broken down and burned."

God heard **Nehemiah's** prayer, and the king didn't get angry. "What do you want me to do?" the king asked.

"Please let me go back to my country and **rebuild** the city where my fathers lived."

"You may go," the king replied.

Now **Nehemiah** was filled with joy. God had protected him from the king's anger. Now he could go back to his home in Israel. He could **rebuild** the city that was destroyed! God's people had sinned, but now God was merciful to His people again. He is a very good God!

And I said: "I pray, Lord God of heaven, O great and awesome God, You who keep Your covenant and mercy with those who love You and observe Your commandments, please let Your ear be attentive and Your eyes open, that You may hear the prayer of Your servant."
(Nehemiah 1:5-6)

Faith Lessons

Nehemiah repented — The land of Israel was destroyed. Its cities were burned down. Nehemiah knew that God had judged His people for their sin. He repented and turned from his sin. He asked God to forgive him. It is good to repent and turn away from our sins. It is good to run to God. He is ready to forgive.

God rules over all people — The king was an enemy of Israel, but he still let Nehemiah go back to build the city. Why did he do this? God rules over all things and all people. He can even make His enemies help His people. God is strong and wise, and He will make all things work for good for His people. He makes even His **worst** enemies serve Him. Let us praise this mighty God!

Vocabulary

Nehemiah	sorrow	worst
cupbearer	rebuild	
rubble	silently	

CHAPTER 41

Nehemiah Rebuilds the Wall

Nehemiah went back to the land of Israel. He went to the biggest city in the land. The city was called Jerusalem. It was a large city, but now it was ruined. The walls were all broken down, and the gates were burned.

Some people lived in the city. There weren't many of them, but a few people from Israel lived there with their families. Nehemiah called these people together. He said, "You see what a mess our city is. Come, let us rise up and rebuild it. Let's build the walls and make new gates."

The people were glad to help. They took their families and started working on the wall. They cleared away the rubble and started building. It was hard work, but they repaired the

wall a little at a time. Even the daughters helped with the work.

But the enemies of Israel saw what the people were doing. They didn't want the city to be rebuilt, so they **plotted** to stop the people. They made a plan to sneak up and attack the people while they were working.

Nehemiah heard about this **plot**. He called the people together and told them what their enemies planned to do. He said, "You must all get a **weapon**. Get your swords and shields. Keep them beside you while you work. Then, if the enemy comes, you can fight them."

There weren't many people in the city. They weren't strong or powerful. But Nehemiah knew that God was strong. He could protect them from their enemies. He said, "Don't be afraid. Remember the Lord. He is strong and mighty. Trust Him, and fight for your families. Fight for your wives and your sons and daughters."

The people obeyed. They kept their swords beside them while they worked. But they didn't have to fight. God protected them from their enemies.

After the people finished building the wall, Nehemiah hung the gates to the city. Then all the people gathered in the open **square**. This was a special place for the people to meet. The men and women and children all stood there. Then Ezra the **scribe** took out the book of the Law. This was the book Moses wrote. It was God's Word. It is in our Old Testament. Ezra read the book of the Law to all the people.

When Ezra finished reading, all the people said, "**Amen**! We will follow this Law. We will serve this God!" Then they bowed down and worshiped the Lord.

The people cried when they heard God's Word. They cried because they knew they had sinned. Now they turned from their sin to serve God. Nehemiah told them, "This is a day of rejoicing. This day is holy to the Lord. Don't cry anymore, for the joy of the Lord is your strength."

Then he said to them, "Go your way, eat the fat, drink the sweet, and send portions to those for whom nothing is prepared; for this day is holy to our Lord. Do not sorrow, for the joy of the LORD is your strength."
(Nehemiah 8:10)

Faith Lessons

The people were happy to work — It was hard work to rebuild the wall, but the people were glad to do it. They were glad to be in their own land. They were glad to serve God. They were glad to work for God and for His people.

God's enemies plot against Him — Many enemies tried to stop the people from building the wall. They made plots and tried to kill them. But God knew what the enemies were planning. He isn't afraid of their plots. He laughs at them because He is strong. He is able to protect His people.

The people repented — The people listened to God's Word. Then they turned from their sins and asked God to forgive them. We must repent like they did. We must turn from our sins and ask God to forgive us.

Vocabulary

Jerusalem	weapon	amen
repair	square	
plot	scribe	

CHAPTER 42

Preparing for the Savior

God judged His people. He destroyed many of them for their sins. But He had mercy on some of them. He didn't forget His promise to Abraham. He promised to bless Abraham's children and make a great nation out of them. He promised to bless all nations of the world through him.

Now some of the people had returned to Israel. They lived in the land again. But they weren't free. They still had many enemies. Their enemies ruled over them. They couldn't fight these enemies. They weren't strong enough to win against them.

The people had an enemy inside them, too. This enemy

was sin. They couldn't beat this enemy, either. It was too strong.

God saw the enemies of His people. He saw the wicked men that ruled them. He also saw the sin inside them. The people couldn't beat these enemies, but God could. He gave His people a promise. When Adam and Eve sinned, God promised to send a Seed to crush the devil. This Seed would

save His people from sin.

Now God **reminded** His people of this promise. He said, "I will send a Man to save My people. I will put My Spirit on Him. I will **anoint** Him to preach good news to the poor. He will heal the brokenhearted. He will free the captives. He will open prison doors and set the prisoners free. He will **proclaim** the year of the Lord. This will be a time when the Lord will show **favor** to His people. He will have mercy on His people and will save them."

The man God promised to send would be a special man. He would be the **Messiah**. **Messiah** means "**anointed** one." An **anointed** person is someone God has chosen for a special job. The **Messiah** would come with a very special job to do. He would come to set the people free from their sin. He would save them and would make them the people of God. This was God's promise. It is a very good promise!

The people were glad to have God's promise. They waited and waited for the **Messiah** to come. One day God would send Him. The people waited and wondered, "Will the **Messiah** come soon?" Yes, God would send Him very soon.

"The Spirit of the Lord G<small>OD</small> *is upon Me,*

Because the L<small>ORD</small> *has anointed Me*

To preach good tidings to the poor;

He has sent Me to heal the brokenhearted,

To proclaim liberty to the captives,

And the opening of the prison to those who are bound;

To proclaim the acceptable year of the L<small>ORD</small>*."*

(Isaiah 61:1-2)

Faith Lessons

God never forgets His promises — God made a promise to Adam and Eve a long, long time ago. But He never forgot this promise. He kept His promise just like He said He would. We can trust God. He always tells the truth and always keeps His promises. Let us praise Him!

The people waited for God — God made a promise, and the people trusted Him. But they had to wait for Him to keep His promise. We must trust God, too. But we must also wait for Him. He will keep His promises, but He will do it in His time.

God sent a Messiah — God's people sinned, but God had grace on them. He promised to send a Messiah to save them from their sins. This is Jesus. Praise God for Jesus! Thank Him for His love and grace!

Vocabulary

remind	brokenhearted	favor
anoint	proclaim	Messiah

CHAPTER 43

God Keeps His Promise

A young woman lived in Israel. Her name was Mary. She lived in a city called Nazareth. One day, she had a very special visitor. The visitor was an angel.

The angel said to Mary, "Don't be afraid, Mary, for you have found favor with God. The Spirit of God is going to come upon you, and you will have a Son. You will call Him Jesus, for He will save His people from their sins. He will be great, and He will reign on the throne of David forever. And His kingdom will never end."

God had promised to send a perfect king to rule on David's throne. He had promised to send a Messiah to save His people from sin. Now He was keeping His promise!

Soon Mary gave birth to a little boy. She named Him Jesus just like the angel told her to.

When Jesus was born, more angels came to announce His birth. People came to worship Him even though He was just a little baby.

But Jesus didn't stay a baby. He grew up into a Man. When he was about thirty years old, He went to the Jordan River. A man named John was preaching at the Jordan River. He was telling the people of Israel to repent of their sins. He told them to turn back to God and follow Him. Then he baptized the people.

Jesus came to the river while John was preaching. John saw Jesus and said, "Look! Here is the Lamb of God who takes away the sin of the world!"

Jesus asked John to baptize Him, so John did.

When Jesus was baptized, the Holy Spirit came down from heaven and rested on Him. All the people saw this and were amazed. Then a voice came from heaven and said, "This is My beloved Son. I am very pleased with Him." God was telling all the people that Jesus was His Son. Jesus is God.

And suddenly a voice came from heaven, saying, "This is My beloved Son, in whom I am well pleased."
(Matthew 3:17)

Faith Lessons

God sent Jesus — God promised to send a king to rule on the throne of David. He promised to send a king whose kingdom would last forever. This kingdom would break all other kingdoms, just like Daniel said. Now God kept His promise by sending Jesus. Jesus is the King who will reign forever, and His kingdom will never end.

We are full of sin — John preached to the people and told them to repent. He told them to turn from their sins. But the people couldn't stop sinning. They needed someone to save them from their sins. Jesus came to do this.

Jesus is God — God promised to send a man to save His people. But no man can save anyone from sin. Only God can do this. Jesus was a Man. But He is also God. He is God and Man together. Praise God for this! He is a very wise and good God!

Jesus is the Lamb of God — When Abraham took Isaac up the mountain to make a sacrifice, Isaac asked, "Where is the lamb?" Abraham said, "God will send a lamb." Now God had sent His lamb. He sent Jesus. Jesus came to die for His people. He is the perfect Lamb of God! Thank God for sending Jesus!

Vocabulary

Nazareth	announce	beloved
visitor	baptize	
angel	amaze	

CHAPTER 44

Will Jesus Sin?

When Jesus was baptized, God spoke from heaven. He told the people that Jesus was His Son. All the people heard this. But the devil heard it, too. He didn't want Jesus to save His people from sin, so he tried to stop Him. He said, "If I can make Jesus sin, then He can't save His people anymore. I will make Him sin!"

Jesus left the Jordan River and went into a desert place. There was nothing to eat there, and Jesus got very hungry. He didn't eat for forty days. Then the devil came to Him. He said to himself, "I will **tempt** Jesus to sin. I will make sin look good to Him. Then maybe He will sin."

The devil said to Jesus, "You're hungry. If You **really** are the Son of God, then You can **perform** a miracle. See these stones? You could turn them into bread if You were **really** God."

But Jesus didn't listen to the devil. He said, "It's **written** in God's Word, 'Man doesn't live by bread only, but by every word of God.'" Jesus knew that people need God's Word even more than they need food. He would obey God, but He

would never obey the devil.

Then the devil tried something new. He took Jesus to Jerusalem. He took Him to the **highest** point on the **temple**. Then he said, "If You are the Son of God, jump off this high place! For God will send His angels to catch You so You don't get hurt. Then You can prove that You **really** are the Son of God. Try it!"

But Jesus said, "God's Word says that we should not **tempt** the Lord our God." God promises to protect His people. But Jesus knew it would be wrong to jump off the **temple** and hope God protected Him. That would be the same as **tempting** God. It's wrong to do foolish things and think God will protect us.

Then the devil took Jesus up to a very high mountain. He showed Him all the kingdoms of the world. There were many powerful kingdoms on the earth, and the devil showed Him all these. Then he said, "These kingdoms are all mine. I'll give them to You if You will worship me."

But Jesus said to him, "Get away from Me, Satan! God's Word says that we must never worship anyone but God. He is the only One we should serve."

Satan had tried to make Jesus sin, but he couldn't. He

tried and tried, but Jesus would not sin. That's because Jesus is God. He is stronger than Satan. He is stronger than all the powers of **wickedness**. He will never sin because He is God.

The devil realized he couldn't make Jesus sin, so he ran away. "I'll try again another time," he said to himself. "Maybe I can make Jesus sin later." Do you think he can?

> *Then Jesus said to him, "Away with you, Satan! For it is written, 'You shall worship the* LORD *your God, and Him only you shall serve.'"*
> *(Matthew 4:10)*

Faith Lessons

Jesus is God — The devil tempted Jesus to sin, but Jesus didn't sin. He is God, and He is perfect. He will never sin. Let us praise God for sending Jesus!

God's Word is our sword — When the devil tempted Jesus to sin, Jesus quoted the Bible. The Bible is a sword. Jesus used it to fight His enemy. It is a very good sword. God has given it to us to use in our battles. We can use it to fight against the devil. We can also use it to fight against our sin. Thank God for giving us the Bible!

The devil will never win — Satan thought he could make Jesus sin. But Jesus won't sin. He is God. The devil is very foolish to think he can make Jesus sin. He is foolish to think he can fight against God and win. One day God will destroy the devil and all his works of wickedness.

Vocabulary

tempt	written	wickedness
really	highest	
perform	temple	

CHAPTER 45

Jesus Teaches in the Synagogue

Jesus went back to Nazareth where He had grown up. On the Sabbath day, He went to the **synagogue**. The **synagogue** was the place where the people of Israel met to worship God. They read from the **Scriptures** and learned about God here.

When it was time to read from the **Scripture**, Jesus stood up to read. He read from a book written by one of the prophets. In this book, God talked about the Messiah who would come to save His people. Jesus read:

> *"The Spirit of the Lord is upon Me,*
> *Because He has anointed Me*
> *To preach the gospel to the poor.*

He has sent Me to heal the brokenhearted,
To proclaim liberty to the captives
And to give sight to the blind.
He has sent Me to free those who are slaves
And to proclaim the year of the Lord."

The people listened as Jesus read to them. Then Jesus said, "Today this Scripture is fulfilled. It is happening right here in front of you."

The people were surprised when He said this. "Isn't this the Man who grew up in our town?" they asked. "He isn't anyone special. We've known Him since He was a boy."

But Jesus said, "No prophet is accepted in his own country." He knew the people wouldn't listen to His words because they thought He was just like them. They didn't believe He was the Son of God. They didn't believe in Him. Then Jesus said, "There were many lepers in Israel when Elisha was alive. But he didn't heal any of them except Naaman, who was a stranger to Israel." Jesus told the people that the men of Israel didn't believe Elisha, either. They rejected the prophets God sent to them. And now they were rejecting Jesus even though God had sent Him, too.

The people were angry when Jesus said this. They said, "Let's kill Him!" They grabbed Jesus and pulled Him up to the top of a hill. They planned to throw Him down from the hill and kill Him. But Jesus escaped from them and got away. Then He left that town and went to another city.

And the eyes of all who were in the synagogue were fixed on Him. And He began to say to them, "Today this Scripture is fulfilled in your hearing."
(Luke 4:20-21)

Faith Lessons

God told His people that Jesus would come — God wrote about Jesus in the Bible long before Jesus ever came to earth. God told His people that He would send a Messiah. This is Jesus.

Jesus came to save His people — Jesus came to preach the gospel. He came to bring good news to His people. He came to heal the hurting. He came to free the captives. He came to give sight to blind people. He came to save His people from sin. Let us praise Him!

The people rejected Jesus — The people didn't believe Jesus. They thought He was a man just like them. They didn't believe He was the Son of God, so they tried to kill Him. We must not be like these people. We must believe what Jesus said. We must trust Him and run to Him to save us.

Vocabulary

synagogue	liberty	accept
Scripture	sight	
gospel	fulfill	

CHAPTER 46

A Roman Soldier Has Faith

Jesus traveled through many cities and **villages**. He preached to the people in Israel. He preached in cities and in fields. Many people came to hear Him. Some listened to Him. These people followed Him and believed Him. But some people didn't like what He said. They didn't believe Him.

Jesus chose twelve men and called them to follow Him. He taught these men and took them with Him when He preached. The men were called His **disciples**. A **disciple** is someone who follows and learns from someone else. These men learned many things from Jesus.

One day Jesus entered a city. A man lived in the city, but

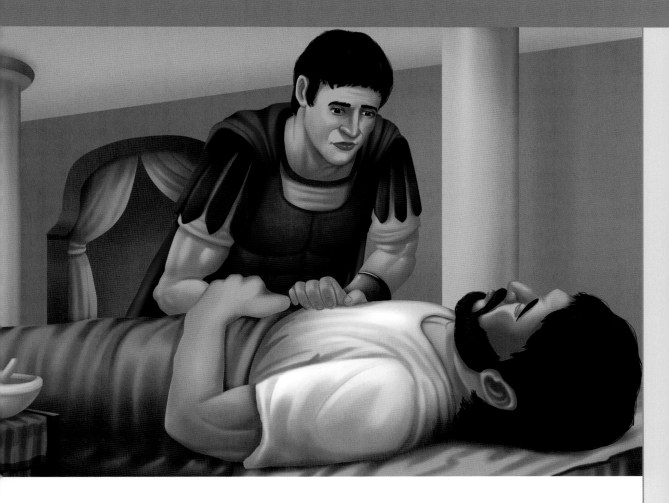

the man wasn't from Israel. He was a Roman soldier. He heard about Jesus, and he believed in Him.

But the soldier had a problem. One of his servants was sick. The man loved his servant very much. He was afraid he would die. No one could help the servant get well. But then the man heard that Jesus had come to his city. "Jesus can make him well!" he thought. So he sent messengers to ask

Jesus to heal his servant.

The **messengers** came to Jesus and told Him about the Roman soldier. "Please help him," they said. "He loves our nation and has helped us. Please heal his servant."

Jesus went with them. A large crowd of people followed Him. Then one of the men ran back to the Roman soldier to tell him that Jesus was coming.

When the soldier heard this, he said to himself, "Jesus can't come to my house! I'm not **worthy** enough to have Him come here. I'm a sinful man, and He is the Lord."

The soldier sent another **message** to Jesus. He said, "Lord, I'm not **worthy** to have You come to my house. Please don't trouble Yourself. Besides, You don't need to come here to heal my servant. You are so powerful that You can just say a word, and my servant will be healed. I'm a soldier, and I have many men working under me. I command them what to do, and they do it. You are the same. You are the Lord over all things. You can command this sickness to leave, and it will leave."

When Jesus heard this, He was very surprised. He turned around to the crowd of people following Him. "I've never seen such great faith, not even in Israel!" He said. The soldier believed Jesus was strong enough to heal his servant. He believed Jesus could do this even from miles and miles away. Jesus told the crowd, "Many people who come from lands far away from Israel will believe in Me. They will be part of God's people. But the people in Israel who don't believe Me will be cast out."

Then Jesus said to the man, "Go back to your house. The servant is healed."

When the man got back to the soldier's house, he saw that the servant was healed just like Jesus said. Jesus had spoken the word, and the sickness left!

"Lord, do not trouble Yourself, for I am not worthy that You should enter under my roof. Therefore I did not even think myself worthy to come to You. But say the word, and my servant will be healed."

(Luke 7:6-7)

Faith Lessons

Jesus is a powerful God — Jesus didn't need to **touch** the sick man to heal him. He just said a word and the sickness left. He is a very powerful God!

The soldier believed Jesus — The Roman soldier believed that Jesus had the power to heal. He trusted Him to heal his servant. Then he sent a **message** to ask Him to heal. We must be like the soldier. We must trust Jesus. Then we must pray to Him. He is a mighty God.

Jesus will call people from all lands — Jesus calls people from all lands and all countries. He brings them to Himself and makes them His people. He is a very good God. Let us praise Him for this!

Vocabulary

village	worthy	touch
disciple	message	
messenger	cast	

CHAPTER 47

Jesus Raises a Dead Man

After Jesus healed the Roman soldier's servant, He went to a new city. This city was called Nain. A large crowd followed Him to the city, and many of His disciples were with Him, too.

When Jesus entered the gates of the city, He saw a large crowd of **mourners**. A young man had just died, and these people were **mourning** for the dead man. They carried a **coffin** with them, and a woman walked beside the **coffin**. She was the mother of the dead man. She was a widow. Her husband had **already** died, and now her only son was dead, too.

When Jesus saw the woman, He was filled with

compassion. She had lost everyone in her family, and now she was all alone. Tears ran down her cheeks as she walked beside her dead son. But Jesus said to her, "Don't **weep**." He didn't want her to cry. He saw how sad she was, but He was about to turn her sadness into joy.

Then Jesus went to the **coffin** and touched it. The men who carried it were shocked that He touched the **coffin**. They stopped walking and looked at Him. What was He

going to do?

Jesus looked at the young man lying dead in the **coffin**. Then He said, "Young man, I say to you, **arise**." Jesus commanded the dead man to get up. But a dead man can't stand up! The people watched in surprise. What do you think happened next?

Suddenly, the dead man sat up. Then he started to speak. He was alive! Jesus had raised him from the dead! He had brought him back to life!

Jesus gave the young man back to his mother. She was filled with joy to see her son alive again.

The crowd was amazed at what Jesus did. They were filled with fear, too. Who was this Man? Why was He so powerful? The people **glorified** God and said, "God has **visited** His people!" Then they told all their friends about the amazing thing Jesus had done.

When the Lord saw her, He had compassion on her
and said to her, "Do not weep."
(Luke 7:13)

Faith Lessons

Jesus is full of compassion — Jesus saw the widow. He knew her husband was dead. He knew she was very sad because her son was dead, too. He looked at her and had compassion. Even though she was a sinful woman, Jesus wanted to help her. He is a very merciful God. He has compassion on the people He created. Let us thank Him for this!

Jesus is God — The widow's son was dead. When someone dies, we can't bring them back to life. But God can. He is a mighty God. He can even make a dead person alive again.

We are like the dead man — The dead man couldn't make himself alive again. He was dead! We are just like him. We are dead because of sin. We can't fix this. But Jesus can fix it. He is God, and He can save us from sin. He can save us just like He saved the man from death and made him alive again.

Vocabulary

mourner   already   glorified
mourn   weep   visited
coffin   arise

CHAPTER 48

Jesus Heals the Blind

News about Jesus **spread** quickly. It **spread** through all the land of Israel. Soon everyone was talking about Him. Who could He be? He healed sick people. He raised the dead. Was He the Son of God?

Some people believed Jesus. They followed Him. They listened to His teaching. Two people who believed Him were blind men. These men couldn't see. They had never seen Jesus, but they knew He could heal them. They believed He was the king God had promised to send. This king would sit on David's throne and rule forever. The blind men followed Jesus and cried out, "Son of David, have mercy on us!"

It was hard for the blind men to reach Jesus. Large crowds

followed Him, and they had trouble finding a way through
the crowds. When Jesus went into a house, they had to find
out which house He had gone into. This was hard to do when
they couldn't see where they were going. But they didn't care.
They knew Jesus could heal them, so they kept trying until
they found Him.

When the two men came into the house, Jesus saw them.

He knew they wanted Him to heal them. "Do you believe I have the power to do this?" He asked them.

"Yes, Lord!" they said. They knew God had promised to send a Messiah. They trusted God to keep His promise. They believed in Jesus.

Jesus saw that the men believed Him. He touched their eyes and said, "You have faith in Me, and I will heal you." Immediately they could see!

Jesus told them not to tell anyone He had healed them. But the men were so excited they spread the news about Him through the whole country!

Jesus went throughout all of Israel and taught the people. He preached the gospel of the kingdom of God and healed the sick. Many people came to hear Him. Many people followed Him, too. Multitudes of people tried to get close enough to hear Him and be healed.

Jesus saw all the people coming to Him. He looked at them and was filled with compassion. They were like sheep wandering around without a shepherd. They were just like sheep who were scattered and weary because no one was leading them. Jesus saw this and told His disciples, "There's a large harvest here. People are waiting to hear about God, but there aren't many people to preach to them. Pray and ask the Lord to send people to work for Him and gather in His harvest."

But when He saw the multitudes, He was moved with compassion for them, because they were weary and scattered, like sheep having no shepherd.
(Matthew 9:36)

Faith Lessons

The blind men trusted Jesus — The men believed Jesus could heal them. They had faith that He was the king God promised to send. We should be like the blind men. We should trust Jesus. He can wash away our sin just like He healed the two blind men. We must trust Him like they did.

Jesus sends preachers to His people — Jesus saw that the people had no one to lead them. He knew they needed to hear the good news about Him. He had compassion on the people and told His disciples to pray for God to send workers to work in God's harvest. We should pray for God to send men to preach the gospel.

Jesus is the Good Shepherd — God promised to send a shepherd to lead and protect His sheep. This shepherd is Jesus Christ. Let us thank God for sending Jesus!

Vocabulary

spread	throughout	harvest
immediately	multitude	
excited	weary	

CHAPTER 49

Parables about God's Kingdom

Large crowds came to hear Jesus teach. Sometimes He preached to them, and sometimes He told them stories. These stories were called parables. A parable is a story that teaches a lesson. One day Jesus told a parable about some bread. He said:

> "The kingdom of heaven is like leaven. Leaven is what makes bread dough grow and rise. A woman was making a loaf of bread, so she took some leaven and mixed it into her bread dough. Then the leaven caused the dough to rise and become a whole loaf of bread."

This story was about bread. But Jesus wasn't really talking

about bread. He was telling people what the kingdom of God was like. It's just like leaven in bread dough.

Then Jesus told another story. This one was about a mustard seed. He said:

"The kingdom of heaven is like a mustard seed. This is the smallest of seeds. A man took one and planted it in his field. Then the seed started to grow. As it grew, it became a tree. Soon it was a huge tree. It got so big that the birds came and made nests in its branches."

God's kingdom is like the mustard seed. It starts out small, but then it grows and grows.

Then Jesus told another parable. This one was about buried treasure! He said:

"The kingdom of heaven is like treasure hidden in a field. A man came and found the treasure. He was very happy and buried it again. Then he went and sold everything he owned. He took the money and bought the field so he could have the treasure."

Jesus wanted people to understand how important the kingdom of heaven was. It was worth more than a buried

treasure! Then Jesus said:

"The kingdom of heaven is like a man looking for beautiful pearls. One day he found the best pearl in the whole world. He was so excited that he ran home and sold everything he owned. Then he came back and bought the pearl."

The kingdom of God is better than the best pearl in the whole world!

"Again, the kingdom of heaven is like treasure hidden in a field, which a man found and hid; and for joy over it he goes and sells all that he has and buys that field."
(Matthew 13:44)

Faith Lessons

God's kingdom is always growing — When leaven is put into bread dough, the bread grows. When a tree is planted, the tree grows bigger and bigger. God's kingdom is the same way. It's always growing. It started out small. Then it grew to fill many lands and many peoples. Now it is filling countries all over the world! God is watching over His kingdom, and He is making it grow. It keeps growing day after day.

We can't always see what God is doing — If we went outside and watched a tree, we couldn't see it grow. But it's still growing even though we can't see it change. If we come back to the same tree in a few years, we'll see how much it has grown. Sometimes the kingdom of God is the same way. We can't always see it growing, but it's still growing anyway.

Following God is the most important thing for us — Jesus told a story about a man who found the best pearl in the whole world. He sold everything so he could buy the pearl. We should be like that man. We should give up everything to follow Jesus. Following God is the most important thing for us. It is worth more than anything else in the whole world.

Vocabulary

parable	mustard	owned
leaven	buried	pearl
dough	treasure	

CHAPTER 50

Jesus Chooses Anyone He Wants

Jesus told the people another parable. This one was about a man who owned a **vineyard**. A **vineyard** is a garden where grapes grow. Jesus said:

The kingdom of heaven is like a man who owned a **vineyard**. He went out **early** in the morning to hire men to work in his **vineyard**. The men agreed to work all day if he would pay them a silver coin for their work.

Later in the morning, the man went back to the city and found more workers. He said to them, "Come work in my **vineyard** today. When the day is over, I will pay you." The men agreed and came to work.

At **lunchtime** the man went out again and hired more

workers. Then he went out in the **afternoon** and hired more. "I will pay you what is right," he told them. The men agreed to work for him.

Finally, when it was almost evening, the man went back to the city again. He found some men standing doing nothing.

"Why are you standing doing nothing?" he asked.

"Because no one hired us," the men said.

"Come work in my **vineyard**. And when the day is over, I will pay you what is right."

The men came and worked. They didn't work for long because it was almost night.

When it was evening time, the owner called the workers. Then he began to pay them for their work. He gave a silver coin to the men who had only worked one **hour**. Then he gave a silver coin to the men who had worked **since lunchtime**.

Finally, the men who had worked all day came up to be paid. They thought, "The owner will pay us more because we worked longer." But the man gave them a silver coin just like all the other workers. This made the men angry. They said, "We worked all day long! Why don't you pay us more than the men who only worked for one **hour**?"

The owner said, "Why are you angry? I haven't done anything wrong. Didn't you agree to work all day for a silver coin? That's what I gave you. Take it and go away. Why should you be angry if I give the other men as much as you? If I want to give them extra, should you get mad? Can't I do what I want with my own money? Why are you angry because I am good to someone else?"

Jesus told this story to the people of Israel. The people were **proud** because God had called them to be His people. They were like the angry men in the story. But Jesus didn't want them to be **proud**. He said, "The first will be last, and the last first." God was going to call many peoples and nations to become His people. These nations would be His special people, and He would be their Father. He is a good and loving God!

> *"I wish to give to this last man the same as to you. Is it not lawful for me to do what I wish with my own things? Or is your eye evil because I am good?"*
> *(Matthew 20:14-15)*

Faith Lessons

God chooses people whenever He wants to — God calls people to become His children. He chooses these people at different times. Sometimes He has mercy on one nation. Sometimes He has mercy on another. We don't know when He will do this. We must pray for Him to call many peoples and nations to come to Him.

We must not be proud — The people of Israel were proud because they knew about God before other people did. We must not be proud if we know about God. We must thank God for having mercy on us. Then we must pray for other people. We should tell them about Jesus, too.

God calls people to come to Him — God is the owner in the story. He called people to come to him. This is what God does. He chooses sinful people and calls them to come to Him. He is a loving God! Let us praise Him!

Vocabulary

vineyard	afternoon	since
early	finally	proud
lunchtime	hour	

CHAPTER 51

Judas Pretends to Love God

One day Jesus called His disciples. He wanted to tell them something important. He came to earth to die for His people, and He wanted to tell them about this. He said, "The Son of Man is going to be killed. Then He will rise from the dead." But His disciples didn't understand.

Many people in Israel came to hear Jesus teach. Some of them didn't like what He said. They didn't like when He talked about their sins. They liked their sins. They didn't want to repent. The **priests** in Israel didn't like Jesus. The leaders didn't like Him, either. They called some people together and had a meeting. They said, "Let's kill Jesus."

The men agreed to kill Jesus, but they didn't know how to do it. How could they capture Him?

One of the disciples of Jesus was a man named Judas. Judas knew the leaders and rulers didn't like Jesus. He knew they wanted to capture Him, so he decided to help them. He decided to betray Jesus. Betray means to hurt a friend by helping an enemy. Judas was going to help the enemies

261

of Jesus. He was going to try to hurt Jesus even though Jesus was his friend.

Judas went to the priests and rulers of Israel. "I can help you capture Jesus," he said.

The priests and leaders of Israel were very excited. "We'll give you a reward if you help us!" they said. "We'll give you money."

Judas was a very greedy man. He loved money, so he said, "How much money will you give me if I help you?"

The priests said, "We'll give you thirty pieces of silver." This was a lot of money, so Judas agreed. Then he went back to Jesus and the other disciples.

Judas didn't tell anyone where he had been. He didn't tell anyone what he was planning to do. The disciples didn't know. They thought Judas was their friend. But Jesus knew. He is God, so He knew what was inside Judas. He knew what was in his heart.

Then one of the twelve, called Judas Iscariot, went to the chief priests and said, "What are you willing to give me if I deliver Him to you?" And they counted out to him thirty pieces of silver.
(Matthew 26:14-15)

Faith Lessons

The priests and leaders of Israel hated God — They didn't want Jesus to talk about their sins. They didn't want to repent or turn from their sins. They hated God. We must not be like them. We must not love our sins. We must turn away from our sins and run to Jesus.

Judas looked like a good man — Judas followed Jesus. He was one of His disciples. He listened to Jesus teach and preach. He spent time with Jesus and said good things about Him. He looked like a good man on the outside. But on the inside, Judas was a wicked man. Some people might look like good people on the outside. But on the inside, they are very wicked. We must not be like Judas. We must not pretend to love God. We must love Him for real. We must love Him with all our heart. We must love Him on the inside and not only on the outside.

Judas loved money — Judas sinned because he loved money. We must not be like him. We must not love money or things in the world. We must love God.

God knows everything — Judas thought no one would know what he had done. But Jesus knew. Judas couldn't hide from

Jesus. Jesus could see inside his heart. He knew he was going to **betray** Him. God knows everything. We can't hide from Him. We can't hide our sins from Him, either.

Vocabulary

priest	betray	greedy
Judas	reward	pretend

CHAPTER 52

Jesus Is the Good Shepherd

J esus preached to the people. He even talked to the priests and leaders who despised and hated Him. One day He told them another story, a story about sheep. When a shepherd takes care of his sheep, he puts them in a safe place during the night. He does this so that wolves and other things can't hurt the sheep. This safe place is called a **sheepfold**. It has a wall **surrounding** it to protect the sheep. Here is the story Jesus told:

"Every sheepfold has a door. But some people don't use the door when they go into the sheepfold. They climb up over the wall or get in another way. These people aren't shepherds. They are thieves and robbers. They come to steal or kill or

destroy the sheep. But the shepherd enters the sheepfold by the door. The sheep hear him calling them, and they immediately recognize his voice. He calls all his sheep by their names because he knows each one of them. Then he leads them out to graze in green pasture. The sheep follow him because they know who he is, and they trust him."

Jesus told this story to the people, but they didn't understand what He was saying. So He explained it to them. He said:

"I am the door of the sheep. If anyone comes in through Me, he will be saved. I am the good shepherd. The good shepherd gives His life for the sheep. A man who isn't a shepherd won't care about the sheep. If he sees a wolf coming, he'll run away and hide. He won't protect the sheep. Then the wolf will kill and scatter the sheep. But I am the good shepherd. I know all My sheep, and I know all their names. I protect them, and I give My life for My sheep."

Then Jesus said, "I have other sheep that aren't here yet. I will call them and will bring them into the sheepfold. They will hear My voice. There will be one flock of sheep, and I will be the shepherd. My Father loves Me because I give My life for the sheep. I will die for the sheep, and then I will rise from the dead. No one takes My life away from Me. I give it because I want to. I have power to do this, and I have power to come back to life again. This is what My Father told Me to do."

"I am the good shepherd; and I know My sheep, and am known by My own. As the Father knows Me, even so I know the Father; and I lay down My life for the sheep."
(John 10:14-15)

Faith Lessons

Sheep need a shepherd — Sheep can't protect themselves. They can't fight a wolf, and they can't **defend** themselves against a **thief** or a robber. They need a shepherd to protect them and care for them. Only a shepherd can keep them safe. We are just like sheep. We can't protect **ourselves**. We can't save **ourselves** from our enemy, sin. We need a good shepherd. We need a perfect shepherd. We need Jesus.

God the Father sent Jesus — God the Father sent Jesus to be the Good Shepherd. Jesus obeyed His Father. Jesus is God. He is also a King who rules. He rules His sheep as their Shepherd. This is the job God the Father gave Him to do.

A sheep follows the shepherd's voice — Sheep **recognize** the voice of their shepherd. They listen to his voice and follow him wherever he leads. **Christians** are like this, too. They hear the words of God and follow Him. This shows that they are sheep. If they don't listen to Him and don't follow Him, they aren't sheep. Are you a sheep? Do you listen to God's words and follow Him?

Jesus has all power — Jesus chose to die. Some people wanted to kill Him, but they couldn't. He was strong enough to stop them because He is God. But He chose to go to the cross and die. He is a loving God who has power over all His world. Let us praise Him!

Vocabulary

sheepfold	recognize	ourselves
surrounding	graze	Christian
thief	defend	

CHAPTER 53

The Last Supper

The time had come for Jesus to die. He knew it was time, so He called His disciples together. He wanted to have a special meal with them before He died. It was time to **celebrate** the **Passover**. This was a feast that Israel **celebrated** every year. Each year they had a special meal and remembered what God did in Egypt. Do you remember what God did? He killed the firstborn sons of Egypt. But he told His people to kill a lamb and spread its blood around their door. Then He would pass over their house and wouldn't kill them. This was a picture of Jesus.

Jesus knew it was time to **celebrate** the **Passover**. After the meal, He would die for His people. He was the true

Lamb of God. His blood would cover His people just like the lamb's blood covered God's people in Egypt. He would die to save His people. He told His disciples He would die and rise from the dead, but they didn't understand.

Jesus and His disciples sat down to eat. While they were eating, Jesus told them, "One of you is going to betray Me."

The men were shocked. They were all friends! Which one of them would be so wicked as to betray Jesus? They all

began to ask Him, "Lord, is it I?"

The disciples didn't know who would betray their Lord, but Jesus knew. He knew what was in each person's heart. He knew what Judas planned to do. He said, "The Son of Man is going to be betrayed. But **woe** to the man who betrays Him! It would have been better for that man if he had never been born!"

Judas heard what Jesus said. After a little while, he got up and left the room. Where do you think he went?

Jesus and the rest of His disciples kept eating after Judas left. They had bread and wine at the table. Jesus took the bread and broke it. Then He gave it to His disciples. He said, "Take and eat. This is My body which is given for you."

Then He took the wine and gave it to them. He said, "Drink from this, all of you. For this is My blood of the new covenant. I will **shed** My blood for the **forgiveness** of sins." Jesus would die so His people's sins could be forgiven.

When the supper was finished, Jesus and His disciples went outside to a garden on the **Mount** of Olives.

Then He took the cup, and gave thanks, and gave it to them, saying, "Drink from it, all of you. For this is My blood of the new covenant, which is shed for many for the remission of sins."
(Matthew 26:27-28)

Faith Lessons

Jesus is the Lamb of God — God told the people of Israel to kill a lamb when they were in Egypt. He wanted to show them that He would set them free. This was a picture of Jesus. He came to be the Lamb of God. He would die to set His people free from sin.

Jesus loves His people — Jesus told His disciples He was going to die. He loved them very much. He would show His great love for them and all His people by dying for them. Let us thank Him for this love. He is a very good God. Let us praise Him!

Jesus knows all things — Jesus knew who would betray Him. He knew what Judas was planning to do. No one else knew, but Jesus knew. He is God, so He can see inside all hearts. He knows everything we think or say or do.

Vocabulary

celebrate	woe	forgiveness
Passover	shed	mount

CHAPTER 54

Jesus Is Betrayed

Jesus and His disciples went to a garden called **Gethsemane** (Geth-se-mu-nee). It was dark, and the men were tired. But Jesus said to His disciples, "Sit here while I go and pray over there." He wanted His disciples to stay awake. He told them, "My soul is filled with sorrow, even to death. Stay here and watch with Me."

Then Jesus went **apart** by Himself and prayed to God the Father. It was time for Him to die for sin. He was going to take the **punishment** His people deserved. God is angry at sinners. He hates sin, and His anger falls on those who sin. Jesus was going to take this anger on Himself. This was a very **difficult** thing to do, so Jesus went off by Himself and prayed to God His Father.

Then Jesus came back to His disciples. He wanted them to stay awake, but they had all fallen asleep. He woke them up and said, "Can't you stay awake with Me for one hour?" This was a hard night for Jesus, and His friends didn't even stay awake to be with Him.

Then Jesus said, "Get up. I am about to be betrayed." Jesus

knew His enemies were coming.

The sun had set, and it was very dark in the garden. Suddenly the disciples saw torches coming near. A large group of men was coming, and the men had swords and clubs. They were sent by the priests and leaders of Israel.

The disciples were afraid when they saw the men with their weapons. Then they saw Judas walking with the men.

Jesus saw Judas, too. He said to him, "Friend, why have you come?" Judas pretended to be a friend, but Jesus knew he was an enemy. He had led the men into the garden to **arrest** Jesus.

The men with the swords came up to Jesus and captured Him. But one of His disciples got angry. His name was Peter. He grabbed a sword and attacked the men. He wanted to protect Jesus. He swung with his sword and cut off one of the men's **ears**.

But Jesus stopped Peter. "Put your sword away," He said. "If I wanted to, I could pray to My Father, and He would send thousands and thousands of angels to fight for Me. But I don't want this." Jesus had come to die for His people. He wanted to die to pay for their sins, so He let the men **arrest** Him. He even healed the man Peter hurt.

When the men **arrested** Jesus, His disciples got scared and ran away. Then the men tied Jesus and took Him to the priests who hated Him.

Then He said to them,
"My soul is exceedingly sorrowful, even to death."
(Matthew 26:38)

Faith Lessons

It is very hard to pay for sin — Sometimes it's easy to sin. But it isn't easy to pay for sin. If we sin, God must judge us. He must send us to hell. It is very, very hard to pay for sin.

Jesus came to die for His people's sin — Jesus loves His people. He knows it is very hard to pay for sin, so He came to pay for His people's sin. He came to rescue them. Now His people don't need to go to hell. Jesus paid for their sin. Now they can love and serve God and live with Him forever. Praise God for His love! Thank Him for sending Jesus!

Jesus is the Lord — Jesus is **all-powerful**. That means He has all power in His hands. He made the world, and He rules the whole world. The men with swords thought they could capture Him, but they didn't have power to capture Him. Jesus could have killed them all. But He didn't. He chose to go with the men and die for His people. He is a powerful, loving God.

Vocabulary

Gethsemane	difficult	all-powerful
apart	arrest	
punishment	ear	

CHAPTER 55

Judas Despairs

Judas saw the men take Jesus away to the priests and leaders who hated Him. He knew they would **murder** Him. When Judas saw this, he became very sad. He knew he had sinned. He knew Jesus was **innocent**.

Judas had sinned. He had done something very, very wrong. He looked at the thirty silver coins the priests gave him. He loved money, but the coins didn't make him happy anymore. He looked at them and felt sick. He had sinned, and this money would never make him happy. It would never wash his sin away.

Judas wished now that he hadn't betrayed Jesus. His **conscience** told him he had done a very wicked thing, so he

took the silver coins and went back to the priests and leaders of Israel. He showed them the money and tried to give it back to them. He said, "I have sinned, and I have betrayed **innocent** blood. I was wrong to treat Jesus like this."

Judas was very sorry for what he had done. But the priests and leaders weren't sorry. "Why should we care if you betrayed an **innocent** person?" they asked. "We don't care what you did. It's your problem!"

Judas was filled with **despair**. He was sad and scared and angry at the same time. He threw the silver coins down on the floor and ran out of the building.

The priests watched Judas run away. Then they picked up the money he had **thrown** on the floor. They didn't care that he sinned. They didn't care that Jesus was **innocent**. They didn't care that they were trying to kill the Son of God. But they did care about the money. They didn't want it to get lost, so they picked it all up and bought some land with it.

Judas ran and ran. He knew he had sinned. He was very sorry he had sinned, but he didn't pray to God. He didn't turn to God. Instead, he was filled with **despair**. He had no hope, so he killed himself.

Then he threw down the pieces of silver in the temple and departed, and went and hanged himself.
(Matthew 27:5)

Faith Lessons

Judas thought money would make him happy — Judas was glad to get the thirty pieces of silver. He thought the money would make him happy, but he was wrong. Money will never make us happy. Sin will never make us happy. It will always make us sad.

Judas didn't come to God — Judas knew he had sinned. He said he was wrong. He even brought the money back to the priests. But he didn't turn back to God. He turned away from his sin, but he didn't turn to God. We can never be saved by just turning away from sin. We must also turn to God and beg Him to forgive us. We must ask Him to give us a new heart so we can love Him. Only He can do this.

God judged Judas — God judged him and sent him to hell. Sin is very wicked, and God will punish people for it. It is very scary to have God judge you for your sin. We must repent and run to God. We must beg Him to forgive us.

The priests didn't care about sin — The priests knew Jesus was innocent. They knew they were wicked. They knew they were sinning. But they didn't care. They rejected God. One day, God would judge them for this.

Vocabulary

murder	conscience	thrown
innocent	despair	scary

CHAPTER 56

Jesus Dies for His Sheep

The men took Jesus to the priests and leaders of Israel. The priests and leaders wanted to kill Him. They knew He was innocent, so they tried to find men who would lie and say Jesus was **guilty**. They called many **witnesses**. These men came and told lies about Jesus. But they couldn't agree with each other. Everyone knew they were lying.

Then the priests sent Jesus to **Pilate**. **Pilate** was the Roman **governor**. He ruled over the people in Jerusalem. The priests hoped **Pilate** would kill Jesus. They told **Pilate**, "Jesus is trying to make Himself into a king. He is a wicked man."

When **Pilate** heard this, he asked Jesus, "Are You a king?"

Jesus said, "You are right to say I am a king. This is why I was born. This is why I came into the world."

Pilate knew Jesus was innocent. He knew the priests and rulers were wrong to try to kill Him. He told them, "Jesus is not **guilty**. He didn't do anything wrong."

But the priests and rulers got angry. "Kill Him!" they shouted.

Pilate was afraid of the people. He didn't want the priests and rulers to get angry at him, so he agreed to kill Jesus. He told his soldiers to beat Jesus. Then he ordered them to take Him away and kill Him.

The soldiers took Jesus to a hill outside the city. They nailed Him to a cross and hung Him there to die.

When the soldiers hung Jesus on the cross, the sun stopped shining. Everything was as dark as night. The people saw this and were afraid. Why had the sun stopped shining?

Then Jesus cried out with a very **loud** voice and died. Suddenly the ground started shaking. It was an **earthquake**! The **earthquake** was so strong that the rocks broke into pieces. The soldiers who stood by the cross were scared. They thought, "God must be angry because we have killed this innocent Man!" One of them said, "**Truly** this was the Son of God!"

That evening, the friends of Jesus came and took His body away. They wrapped it up and put it in a **tomb**. The **tomb** was a cave. After they put the body inside, someone rolled a large stone over the door of the **tomb**.

The disciples of Jesus were very sad. They thought Jesus

was their Messiah. They thought He would be a king and rule over them forever. They thought He was the man God had promised to send. But now He was dead. They didn't understand. They didn't know why He had died.

> *Pilate therefore said to Him, "Are You a king then?"*
> *Jesus answered, "You say rightly that I am a king. For this cause*
> *I was born, and for this cause I have come into the world."*
> *(John 18:37)*

Faith Lessons

God had a plan — The disciples didn't understand why Jesus died, but God did. He had a plan. He sent Jesus to die. This was His plan all the time. He worked His plan even by using wicked people. He used the priests and rulers who hated Jesus. He used the men who lied about Jesus. He used Pilate who sent Jesus to die. God rules His world, and He uses all His world to work His good plan. He is a wise and mighty God. Let us praise Him!

God kept His promise — God made a promise to His people. He kept His promise when He sent Jesus. Jesus was the Seed God promised Adam and Eve. He was the king God promised David. He was the Messiah God promised to send to save His people. God always keeps His promises! All His promises are fulfilled in Jesus! Let us thank Him for this!

Jesus died for sinners — The disciples were afraid. They ran away when wicked men came to take Jesus. But Jesus still loved them. They were full of sin, but Jesus never stopped loving them. He loves His people, and He came to die for them even though they are sinful. Praise Him for His love!

Vocabulary

guilty	governor	truly
witness	loud	tomb
Pilate	earthquake	

CHAPTER 57

Jesus Defeats Sin and Death

For three days the body of Jesus lay in the tomb. His disciples were filled with sorrow. Then, on **Sunday** morning, some of the women who believed in Jesus came to the tomb. They brought **spices** to anoint His body. But when they got to the tomb, they got a big surprise. The tomb was empty! The stone was rolled away from the door, and Jesus was gone!

The women ran into the tomb and looked around. Suddenly they saw two angels standing beside them. The angels were dressed in shining clothes. The women were terrified. They fell to the ground, but the angels told them not to be afraid.

"Why are you looking for a living person in a dead man's tomb?" the angel asked. "The Man you're **seeking** isn't here. Jesus has **risen**!"

Then the angel said, "Don't you remember that He told you He was going to die? He said that sinful men would kill Him, and then He would rise from the dead."

Suddenly the women remembered Jesus had told His disciples this. They had forgotten His words, but now they remembered.

The angel said, "Go quickly and tell His disciples that He

is **risen** from the dead."

The women ran out of the tomb and raced toward the city. They were **astonished** at what they had seen. They were very surprised at what the angel told them. But they were filled with joy, too.

While they were running, Jesus suddenly came to them. "Hello," He said. The women fell down in front of Jesus and worshiped Him. He was alive!

That night, the disciples were gathered together in a room. It was **Sunday** evening, and they were hiding because they were afraid the priests and rulers of Israel would come to kill them, too. They had locked the door of the room they were in, but suddenly Jesus came in. "Peace be to you," He said.

The disciples were **astonished** to see Jesus. He showed them His hands and feet where He had been **wounded** when He died on the cross. "See My hands and feet," He said. "I'm really here. It's really Me."

The disciples were filled with joy. Jesus was alive!

They said to them, "Why do you seek the living among the dead? He is not here, but is risen!"

(Luke 24:5-6)

Faith Lessons

Jesus rose from the dead — Jesus died for the sins of His people. But He didn't stay dead. After three days, He rose from the dead. Now He is alive. We call this the resurrection.

Jesus is Lord over all things — Jesus died. But He is God the Lord, so death has no power over Him. He didn't stay in the grave. He came back to life by His own power. He rules all things and all the world. Let us praise Him! Let us worship Him!

Jesus rose from the dead on Sunday — Sunday is the day our Lord Jesus rose from the dead. This day is called the Lord's Day. This is the day we meet together at church to worship God and to remember His resurrection.

Vocabulary

Sunday	risen	resurrection
spice	astonished	
seek	wounded	

CHAPTER 58

Thomas Learns to Believe

The disciples of Jesus were filled with joy when they saw He was still alive. But one of the disciples didn't know Jesus was alive. His name was Thomas. Thomas wasn't with the disciples on Sunday night when Jesus came to them.

Later on, Thomas came to the other disciples. They told him, "We have seen the Lord!"

But Thomas didn't believe them. "Jesus can't be alive!" he thought. "He's dead!"

The disciples tried to convince him that Jesus was alive, but Thomas wouldn't believe it. He was full of doubt. Could Jesus really rise from the dead?

Thomas said, "I don't believe it. Unless I see Jesus with my own eyes, I won't believe. Unless I can put my finger in the nail holes in His hands where He hung on the cross, I won't believe He's alive!"

A whole week went by. Then, on the next Sunday, all the disciples got together again. Thomas was with them this time. Suddenly, Jesus came into the room and said, "Peace be to you."

The disciples rejoiced to see their Lord again. But Jesus turned to Thomas. He knew what Thomas had said. Even though Jesus wasn't present when Thomas talked to the disciples, He knew everything Thomas had said. How did He know? He is God!

Jesus knew Thomas didn't believe, so He said to him, "Come here, Thomas. See My hands? Come put your finger in the nail holes in My hands. Do you see the wound in My side? Come touch it. Don't be unbelieving, and don't doubt. Believe in Me."

Thomas saw Jesus and knew he was wrong to doubt. He worshiped Jesus and said, "You are my Lord and my God!"

Jesus said, "Thomas, you believe because you have seen Me. But blessed are those who have not seen Me and yet still believe."

Another disciple was named John. John wrote a book about Jesus. It is called the Gospel of John, and it's part of our Bibles. John wrote down many things Jesus did. He also wrote about Thomas and his doubt. Then John said, "Jesus did many other signs. He did many things that aren't written down. But I wrote these things down so that you can believe that Jesus is the Christ, the Son of God. For, if you believe, you will have life in His name."

Let us believe!

Jesus said to him, "Thomas, because you have seen Me, you have believed. Blessed are those who have not seen and yet have believed."

(John 20:29)

Faith Lessons

The disciples were filled with joy — Jesus is alive! This filled the disciples with joy. It should fill us with joy, too. Let us worship our risen Lord!

Jesus brought peace to His people — Jesus said, "Peace be to you." He brings peace to all who love and obey Him. Let us thank Him for this!

Thomas doubted — Thomas didn't believe Jesus was alive. We don't need to doubt like Thomas did. We must believe God. We must trust in Jesus.

God gave us His Word so that we can believe — God used men to write down His Word, the Bible. He did this so that we could believe in Him. His Word is always true because He wrote it. He will never lie, and His Word will never lie. Let us believe Him, and let us believe His holy Word!

Vocabulary

Thomas	doubt	unbelieving
convince	present	sign

CHAPTER 59

Jesus Returns to Heaven

After He rose from the dead, Jesus met with His disciples many times. He taught them more about Himself. He showed them that the whole Bible talks about Him.

Jesus also said He would send the Holy Spirit. The Spirit would teach His people to understand the Bible. His disciples **marveled** at this. They were amazed that the whole Bible told them about Jesus. For forty days, they learned many things from Him.

Many people saw Jesus during this time. Over five hundred people met to hear Him teach. They were very glad to see Him. He was alive! He had risen from the dead! He was the Son of God!

One day, the disciples met with Jesus again. They worshiped Him. Then Jesus gave them a command. He said to them, "God has given Me all authority. I possess all power. I rule all things. I rule both in heaven and on earth. God the Father sent Me. Now I am sending you. I am sending you into all the world. Go and make disciples of all nations. Teach people to obey all things I have commanded you. Baptize them in the name of the Father and the Son and the Holy Spirit."

Then Jesus said, "I am always with you, forever."

After He said this, Jesus rose up into the sky. He ascended up into heaven. The disciples were startled. They watched as He went up above them. He went up higher and higher into the sky. Then a cloud came across the sky. It hid Jesus so they couldn't see Him anymore.

Now Jesus was gone. But the disciples kept looking up into the sky. They didn't know what to do. Then they saw two angels standing beside them. The angels said, "Men, why are you staring up into the sky? Jesus has gone into heaven. But one day He will come again. He will come back just like you saw Him depart."

The disciples believed the angels. They praised and worshiped God. Then they went back to Jerusalem. They were filled with great joy. They read the Bible and prayed together. They also went to the temple, the house of God. They gathered there to praise and bless God for all that He had done.

And Jesus came and spoke to them, saying, "All authority has been given to Me in heaven and on earth. Go therefore and make disciples of all the nations, baptizing them in the name of the Father and of the Son and of the Holy Spirit, teaching them to observe all things that I have commanded you; and lo, I am with you always, even to the end of the age." Amen.
(Matthew 28:18-20)

Faith Lessons

Jesus has all authority — He has all power. He rules all things in heaven and on earth. He is King of all the world, and He holds all power in His hands. Let us worship and fear this mighty God! Let us praise this ruling King!

Jesus sent His people to teach all nations — Jesus wants His people to go into all the world and teach all peoples about Him. This is His command. He wants all nations to know His good news. This good news is the gospel. He is a good God! He brings good news to the world!

One day Jesus will come back — Jesus went up into heaven. But one day He will come back. He will come to judge the world. He is Lord of all! Let us worship Him!

Vocabulary

marvel	ascend	depart
authority	startled	
possess	higher	

CHAPTER 60

God Sends the Holy Spirit

Before Jesus left, He told His disciples that He would send Someone to them. He called this Person the **Comforter**. This was the **Holy Spirit**. Jesus promised to send Him. The **Holy Spirit** is God just like Jesus is God. He comes to teach His people about Jesus.

Jesus told His disciples, "Do you remember John? John baptized people with water. But I will send the **Holy Spirit** to you. He will baptize you in a different way. After I leave, He will come. He will come soon."

After Jesus left, the disciples went into a room. They met here with many people who believed in Jesus. There were over one hundred people there. They all prayed together.

Suddenly, a loud sound came from heaven. What was it? It sounded like a strong, rushing wind. It filled the whole house. Then something that looked like flames of fire appeared. It rested on the heads of the disciples. Suddenly, the disciples began talking in different languages. The Holy Spirit filled them, and they started preaching in different languages. Jesus had sent the Holy Spirit just like He promised!

Many people from all over the world were nearby. They lived in the city. Now they heard the disciples preaching in their own languages. The people said, "These men are all from Israel. But they're talking in different languages. How did they learn to speak like this? They are telling us all about the wonderful works of God!"

The people were shocked. They didn't know what to think. They said, "What can this mean? How did these men learn to speak like this? How did they learn these things?"

Then Peter stood up. Peter was one of the disciples. He said, "Listen to me, all you people! Jesus lived among you. But you didn't believe Him. You killed Him. But God raised Him back to life. He couldn't stay dead because He is perfect. He is God! He went up into heaven. Now He is sitting at the right hand of God. But He promised to send the Holy Spirit. The Spirit has come. This is why we are speaking like we are. Jesus sent us to tell you the good news about Him."

When the people heard Peter, they were scared. They had killed Jesus. Now they knew they had sinned. But what could they do? They trembled. Then they asked Peter, "What can we do?"

Peter said, "Repent! Turn from your sins. Run to Jesus!

Ask Him to forgive your sins. Then come and be baptized. He will send the **Holy Spirit** to you, too. He will have mercy on you just like us. He has promised this, and He will keep His promise. This good news is for you and your children. God will keep this promise to as many people as He calls."

Peter preached for a long time. The people listened to him. They were glad to hear his words. They turned from their sins. They prayed to Jesus. That day, about three thousand people were saved!

> *Then Peter said to them, "Repent, and let every one of you be baptized in the name of Jesus Christ for the remission of sins; and you shall receive the gift of the Holy Spirit."*
> *(Acts 2:38)*

Faith Lessons

Jesus sent the Holy Spirit — Jesus promised to give a comforter to His people. This is the Holy Spirit. He opens our hearts and minds. He teaches us about Jesus. He teaches us how to understand the Bible. Praise God for sending Him!

The Holy Spirit called people to Jesus — We can't see the Holy Spirit. But He is working. When Peter preached, the Holy Spirit touched the hearts of the people listening. He led the people to Jesus. He opened people's eyes to see the truth about God. Let us praise Him!

Jesus keeps His promises — Jesus is God. When He makes a promise, He will keep it. We can always trust His promises. Let us worship Him!

Vocabulary

comforter	language	among
Holy Spirit	wonderful	tremble

CHAPTER 61

God Uses Peter and John to Heal

Peter and the other disciples preached and preached. They told many people about the good news of Jesus. Peter and some of the disciples were called apostles.

One day, Peter and John went to the temple to pray. Many, many people came to the temple each day. When they came into the temple, they walked past a man sitting on the ground. This man was lame. Lame means he was hurt so he couldn't walk. His feet and ankles were badly hurt, so he couldn't walk at all. He had always been lame ever since he was born. He had never been able to walk. People carried him to the temple every morning, and he sat at the gate and asked for money. He was a beggar.

When Peter and John walked into the temple, the lame man asked them for money. Peter looked at the man and saw he couldn't walk. He said, "Look at us." The lame man looked up at Peter and John. He thought they would give him some money.

But Peter said, "I don't have any money to give you. But I will give you what I do have. In the name of Jesus Christ, I command you to rise up and walk!"

Then Peter took the man's hand and lifted him up. Suddenly, the man's feet and ankles were healed. He could walk! He was so excited that he started running and jumping and praising God. God had healed him!

People all over the temple heard the man shouting and praising God. They looked around and saw him walking and leaping. "Isn't that the lame man?" they asked. They were filled with amazement when they saw him. "Peter and John healed him!" someone shouted. Then all the people ran to see. They surrounded Peter and John.

But Peter said, "Why are you people surprised? Don't look at us. We didn't heal this man by our own power. We couldn't make this man walk by our own godliness. We are sinners just like you are. Jesus is the One who healed Him.

God promised Abraham, Isaac, and Jacob that He would send Jesus. But when He came, you killed Him. Then He rose from the dead, and we have come to tell you about Him. He is the one who healed this man and made him strong so he can walk. It is through faith in Jesus that he has been healed."

Then Peter said, "You people didn't know that Jesus is God. You didn't understand. But now you must repent. You must turn from your sins and be **converted**. You must run to Jesus to save you so that your sins can be washed away. God sent Him to earth to bless you and to wash away your sins."

"To you first, God, having raised up His Servant Jesus, sent Him to bless you, in turning away every one of you from your iniquities."

(Acts 3:26)

Faith Lessons

God healed the lame man — Peter and John saw the lame man and told him to get up and walk. But they didn't heal him. They knew Jesus had the power to heal the lame man, but they didn't. It was God's power that healed him.

Peter and John trusted God — They believed Jesus had all power in heaven and on earth. They had faith that He was strong enough to heal the lame man. We must trust God like they did.

Peter asked the people to repent — Peter told the people about their sins. Then he told them to repent of their sins and turn to God. Peter knew he couldn't make them repent. Only God can do this. But Peter still preached to them just like Jesus told him to.

Vocabulary

apostle	beggar	converted
lame	amazement	
ankle	godliness	

CHAPTER 62

The Rulers Get Angry at Peter and John

The people listened to Peter preach. They saw the lame man healed, and they believed in Jesus. Thousands of people were saved that day. But the priests and rulers of Israel heard about what Peter and John were doing. They heard Peter preaching about Jesus. This made them angry, so they arrested Peter and John.

Then all the rulers and priests got together. They said to Peter and John, "Who told you that you could heal that man? Who gave you the power to do it?"

Peter and John looked around at all the priests and rulers. These were the same people who had killed Jesus. Now they were angry at Peter and John. Would they kill them, too? Do you think Peter and John were afraid? Would you be afraid?

Peter looked at the men and began to answer their question. He wasn't afraid of them. The Holy Spirit filled him and gave him **boldness** to speak to the rulers. God was with him, so he wasn't afraid. He said, "If you are judging us because we healed a **helpless** man, I will tell you how we did it. We didn't heal him. Jesus did. He is the Messiah, and you killed Him. But God raised Him from the dead. Jesus' power healed this man. He is the Lord, and no one can be saved without Him. We can't have **salvation** through anyone except Him!"

The rulers and priests listened as Peter spoke. They were shocked that he was so brave. He was only a **fisherman**, but he wasn't afraid of them! This was a big surprise. Why wasn't he afraid? They thought, "He must be brave because he was with Jesus."

The rulers were afraid to punish Peter and John. They were afraid the crowd would get angry if they did. So they said, "Peter, John, don't ever preach about Jesus again. If you do, we will punish you. Stop preaching!"

Peter said, "You are rulers, and we are supposed to obey you. But we have to obey God first. God told us to preach,

so we will preach. We can't obey you if you tell us to do something wrong. We have to tell people what we know about Jesus!"

The rulers didn't like this answer. They said, "Stop preaching! We're giving you a warning. If you don't stop, you'll be punished!" Then they let them go.

Peter and John went back to the other disciples. They

told them what had happened, and they told them about the **warning** the rulers gave them.

All the disciples got together and prayed. They said, "Lord God, You made heaven and earth and the sea and everything in it. You have all power. These people are fighting against You. They are fighting against Your Son Jesus. Look at their **threats**, and please give us **boldness**. Let us be brave to preach Your Word. Let us be brave to teach all people about You."

When they finished praying, the house shook, and the Holy Spirit filled them. God gave them **boldness** to preach about Him. He heard their prayer, and He answered.

"Nor is there salvation in any other, for there is no other name under heaven given among men by which we must be saved."
(Acts 4:12)

Faith Lessons

The rulers hated God — The rulers and priests tried to stop Peter and John. They hated Jesus, so they hated the people who followed Him. Wicked men will always hate God's ways. They will hate God's people, too. But God is stronger than all wicked people. He is not afraid of them, and we must not be afraid of them, either.

We can only be saved through Jesus — All people have sinned. We can't save ourselves from our sins. No one can save us except Jesus. He is the only One who brings salvation. If we don't run to Him, we will never be saved. Nothing else can ever save us.

Peter and John obeyed God — The rulers told them to do something wrong. They told them to stop preaching. Peter and John knew they had to obey God first. They couldn't obey the rulers and do something wrong. They had to obey God.

Vocabulary

question   salvation   threat
boldness   fisherman
helpless   warning

CHAPTER 63

Stephen Dies for Christ

One of the disciples was named Stephen. He was a man full of faith. He trusted God and preached to the people. He did many wonders among the people. He was a mighty man of God.

Wicked men didn't like Stephen. They didn't like him to preach to the people, so they started arguing with him. They thought they could prove that what he said was wrong. They tried and tried, but Stephen spoke with the wisdom of God. He preached the truth. Nobody could argue against him. Then the men hired people to lie about Stephen. They lied and said he was a rebel and a wicked man.

The rulers and priests arrested Stephen. "Are these things

true?" they asked him.

Stephen said, "Men of Israel, God called our father Abraham. He led him to a new land and blessed him. Abraham didn't have a son, but God promised to give him one. God kept this promise. He gave him Isaac. Later on, when Joseph was a young man, his brothers hated him and sold him as a slave. Joseph lived in Egypt, but God was

with him and delivered him. He made him a ruler, and he protected his **entire** family."

Stephen said, "Later, the king of Egypt tried to kill all the baby boys of Israel. He made the people slaves. Then God called Moses and set His people free. The people **rebelled** against Moses. They didn't want to follow him, but he was the man God chose. He brought the people out of Egypt. Yet the people didn't follow God. They sinned and served false gods. Then God led the people into the promised land. He gave them David, a good king. But the people kept sinning. God sent prophets to tell the people to repent, but they didn't listen."

Then Stephen told the rulers and priests, "You are a **stubborn** people just like your fathers! You always **resist** the Holy Spirit! You act just like the wicked men who lived in Israel before you. God promised to send Jesus, and now you have killed Him. God gave you His Word, and you rejected it!"

When the rulers and priests heard this, they knew it was true. But they didn't want to hear the truth. It made them very angry, so they said, "Let's kill him!" They grabbed Stephen and dragged him out of the city. Then they threw big stones at him and killed him.

As he died, Stephen prayed, "Lord Jesus, receive my spirit. Please, forgive them for this sin." Then he died.

And they stoned Stephen as he was calling on God and
saying, "Lord Jesus, receive my spirit."
(Acts 7:59)

Faith Lessons

Stephen was a man of faith — He wasn't afraid to preach to the people. He wasn't afraid of his enemies. He was a brave, bold man. He did many mighty things. He boldly told others about Jesus.

God works through history — Stephen reminded the people of what God had done for them. God chose and blessed His people for many, many years. Stephen gave them a history lesson. He showed them what God did. It is good to study the works of God in history. It is good to learn what He has done.

Wicked men killed Stephen — Stephen was a righteous man, but wicked men killed him. People are sinful and do very bad things. But God rules over all things, even wicked people. He will use even wicked men to glorify Himself. He used Stephen's death to bring more people to Jesus. He is very wise. And He is very powerful. Let us praise Him!

Vocabulary

Stephen	rebel	resist
arguing	entire	receive
prove	stubborn	

CHAPTER 64

God Sends His Word to the Nations

Cornelius (Cor-neel-yus) was a man in the Roman army. He was not from Israel. He was a leader in the army. He led men to fight in Rome's battles. But he was also a godly man. He feared God and worshiped Him. He taught his family about God. He prayed to God, and he wanted to learn more about Him.

One day an angel came to Cornelius. He said, "God has heard you. Now go ask Peter to come here. He will teach you more about God."

Cornelius was very excited to hear this. He sent someone to ask Peter to come. Then he called all his family together. He called his friends, too. "Someone is coming to teach us

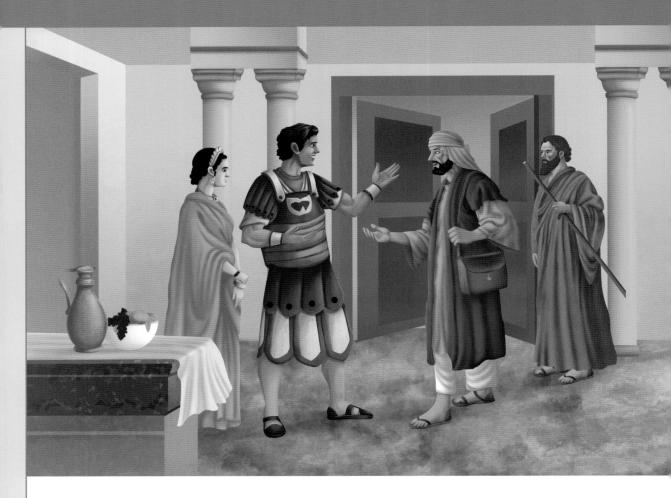

more about God!" he said.

Peter was staying in a town called Joppa. He was telling the people about God. But he was only telling the people of Israel about God. "I am part of God's people," he thought. "I am part of Israel. I am different from other people. I won't even eat with people who aren't from Israel."

But God told him, "I made all people, Peter. I want you to

tell all people about Me. You are all the same because I made all of you."

Suddenly, Peter heard a knock at the door. Men from Cornelius had come, and they were looking for him. These men were not from Israel, but God told Peter, "Go with them. I have sent them." So Peter went.

When Peter got to the house, he saw a large crowd waiting for him. Cornelius saw Peter and worshiped him. But Peter said, "Don't worship me! I'm a man just like you are! Now tell me why you asked me to come."

Cornelius said, "An angel told me that you could teach us more about God. We are all here waiting for you. Please teach us."

Then Peter said, "I thought God only wanted me to teach the people of Israel. But now I see I was wrong. God made all people, and He chooses men and women from all nations to be His people. He sent Jesus, who is Lord of all the world. Wicked men killed Him, but God raised Him up from the dead on the third day. We saw this happen, and He sent us to tell everyone about it. He commanded us to preach to all people. Jesus is the Lord, and He will judge all people who are alive and who are dead. But whoever believes in Him will be saved."

While Peter was speaking, God touched the people who were listening to him. The Holy Spirit fell on the people just like He did on the disciples. Peter was surprised to see God touch people who weren't from Israel. He said, "God had mercy on these people just like He had mercy on us!"

Now Peter knew that God chooses people from every nation in the whole world!

> *Then Peter opened his mouth and said: "In truth I perceive that God shows no partiality. But in every nation whoever fears Him and works righteousness is accepted by Him."*
>
> *(Acts 10:34-35)*

Faith Lessons

God chooses people from every nation — Cornelius was a soldier in the Roman army, but God chose him. He chooses people in every nation all over the world. He chooses anyone He wants. God is sovereign. He has power over all people, and He picks whoever He wants to.

Peter didn't want to be worshiped — Cornelius thought he should worship Peter. But Peter was a man just like any other man. He knew it was wrong to be worshiped. We should only worship God. Peter taught this to Cornelius. God is the only God. We must worship Him alone.

God sent a preacher — Cornelius and his family needed to learn about God, so God sent a preacher to them. He sent Peter to teach the people. God uses preachers to speak His word to people. We should pray for our preachers. We should also ask God to raise up more preachers to preach His word.

Vocabulary

Cornelius	third	sovereign
knock	whoever	preacher

CHAPTER 65

Paul Preaches Truth to the Greeks

Paul was an apostle who was sent by Jesus. He went to many towns and cities to preach. He taught people in Israel and in other lands and nations. One day he went to Athens, a city in Greece. This was a city where Greek people lived. These people worshiped idols and served gods that weren't really gods. Paul was filled with grief and sorrow when he saw this. He talked to the people and told them about the true God. He explained who Jesus was and begged the Greeks to repent and turn away from their sins.

The people listened as Paul preached. "What is he saying?" they asked. "He's telling us about a strange new god."

The people wanted to hear about this new god, so they

gathered together to hear Paul preach. "What is this new teaching?" they asked **eagerly**. "We want to know what you're talking about."

Paul stood up in front of the people and said, "Men of **Athens**, I see that you are very **religious**. You spend a lot of time worshiping and sacrificing to your gods. You even made an altar to a god you don't know anything about. You call this god 'the **unknown** god,' and I have come to tell you about a God you don't know yet."

Then Paul said, "God made the world and everything in it, so He is Lord of heaven and earth. He owns all things and rules all things. He made all people on earth from one man and one woman. He put all people on earth, and He chooses where they each will live. He rules over all people, and all people must worship and serve Him. We must not make **idols** or statues of God. We must worship the true God. He commands us to repent and turn from our sins. We must turn to Him and fear and love Him. Jesus came to die, and He rose from the dead. One day He will come back to judge the whole world."

The people were surprised to hear what Paul said. They responded to him in different ways. Some of them believed his words. They repented of their sins and turned to God. But other people didn't believe, and they **mocked** Paul. "You're silly to believe this!" they said. Other men said, "We want to think about this, and then we will talk to you again."

Paul was glad to preach to the people. He knew God could save the **Greeks**. God has power to change the hearts of sinful people. He is a mighty God!

"God, who made the world and everything in it, since He is Lord of heaven and earth, does not dwell in temples made with hands. Nor is He worshiped with men's hands, as though He needed anything, since He gives to all life, breath, and all things. And He has made from one blood every nation of men to dwell on all the face of the earth."

(Acts 17:24-26)

Faith Lessons

Paul preached the truth — Paul told the Greeks about God, and he told them about their sin, too. He preached the truth to the people. Some people got angry, but Paul still preached. We must be like him. We must speak the truth even if people get angry. We must always obey God and speak the truth.

God is the Lord of all people — God made Adam and Eve. All people on earth came from Adam and Eve's children. God made all these people, and He rules over all of them. All people must worship God. We must all repent and turn to Jesus, for He is Lord of all!

Jesus is the Shepherd — Jesus has a flock. This flock is His people. He calls people from all nations all over the world to be part of His flock. Then He makes them all one people in Him. All Christians are part of one church in Jesus Christ. He is their Lord and Shepherd.

Vocabulary

Athens	idol	religious
Greece	grief	unknown
Greek	eagerly	mock